## About the Center for Creative Leadership

The Center for Creative Leadership is an international, nonprofit, educational institution whose mission is to advance the understanding, practice, and development of leadership for the benefit of society worldwide. Founded in Greensboro, North Carolina, in 1970 by the Smith Richardson Foundation, Inc., the Center is today one of the largest institutions in the world focusing on leadership. In addition to locations in Greensboro; Colorado Springs, Colorado; San Diego, California; and Brussels, Belgium, the Center maintains relationships with more than twenty network associates and partners in the United States and abroad.

The Center conducts research, produces publications, and provides a variety of educational programs and products to leaders and organizations in the public, corporate, educational, and nonprofit sectors. Each year through its programs, it reaches more than twenty-seven thousand leaders and several thousand organizations worldwide. It also serves as a clearinghouse for ideas on leadership and creativity and regularly convenes conferences and colloquia by scholars and practitioners.

For more information on the Center for Creative Leadership, call Client Services at (336) 545-2810, send an e-mail to info@leaders.ccl.org, or visit the Center's web site at http://www.ccl.org.

Funding for the Center for Creative Leadership comes primarily from tuition, sales of products and publications, royalties, and fees for service. The Center also seeks grants and donations from corporations, foundations, and individuals in support of its educational mission.

Center for
**Creative Leadership**

leadership. learning. life.

# Wilfred Drath

# The Deep Blue Sea

## Rethinking the Source of Leadership

Center for
**Creative Leadership**

leadership. learning. life.

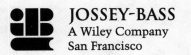

JOSSEY-BASS
A Wiley Company
San Francisco

Published by

**JOSSEY-BASS**
A Wiley Company
350 Sansome St.
San Francisco, CA 94104-1342

www.josseybass.com

Jossey-Bass books and products are available through most bookstores. To contact Jossey-Bass directly, call (888) 378-2537, fax to (800) 605-2665, or visit our website at www.josseybass.com.

Substantial discounts on bulk quantities of Jossey-Bass books are available to corporations, professional associations, and other organizations. For details and discount information, contact the special sales department at Jossey-Bass.

We at Jossey-Bass strive to use the most environmentally sensitive paper stocks available to us. Our publications are printed on acid-free recycled stock whenever possible, and our paper always meets or exceeds minimum GPO and EPA requirements.

**Library of Congress Cataloging-in-Publication Data**

Drath, Wilfred H.
   The deep blue sea : rethinking the source of leadership / by
Wilfred H. Drath.
          p. cm.—(Jossey-Bass business & management series)
"A Joint Publication of The Jossey-Bass Business & Management
Series and The Center for Creative Leadership."
Includes bibliographical references and index.
   ISBN 0-7879-4932-9
   1. Leadership.   I. Title.   II. Series.
HD57.7 .D73 2001
   658.4'092—dc21                                          00-011520

FIRST EDITION
*HB Printing*   10 9 8 7 6 5 4 3 2 1

A Joint Publication of

The Jossey-Bass

Business & Management Series

and

The Center for Creative Leadership

*To my mother and father*
*and to*
*Linda*
*and to*
*Will, Alice, and Bess*

# Contents

Acknowledgments      xi

*Introduction*      xiii

1. Leadership Principles and Leadership Tasks      1

2. Personal Dominance      31

3. Interpersonal Influence      63

4. The Limits of Interpersonal Influence      93

5. Relational Dialogue      125

Epilogue: A New World for Zoffner Music      167

*Bibliography*      175

*Index*      177

*About the Author*      187

# Acknowledgments

This book has involved the extraordinary talents and caring of the people of the Center for Creative Leadership and many others both outside the CCL family and former members of it. I cannot possibly mention everyone who has played a role, but I desire to acknowledge those friends and colleagues most closely connected to this work.

The place of honor is reserved for Chuck Palus, my closest colleague and friend, whose abiding, inquiring, appreciative, doubting, joyous spirit and intelligence I have leaned on and learned from over and over again. Thanks is way too small a word, Charles, but thanks anyway.

Also deeply important in my development is Bob Kaplan, who, years ago as I was just emerging as a professional in this field, challenged and supported me in learning to work hard, become committed, and think for myself.

This book would not exist without the ideas of writers who have inspired me and whose work I have drawn on heavily: Michael Basseches, Jerome Bruner, Mary Parker Follett, Kenneth Gergen, Nelson Goodman, Ronald Heifetz, Robert Kegan, Charles Palus, Karl Weick, and Etienne Wenger.

In addition, I am in the debt of colleagues—some of whom gave me invaluable feedback on the manuscript—whose ideas, questions, and conversation have contributed significantly: Robert Burnside, Maxine Dalton, David Day, Nancy Dixon, Chris Ernst, Bob Goodman, Michael Hoppe, Marcia Horowitz, David Horth, David Hurst, Kenton Hyatt, Winn Legerton, Cindy McCauley,

Russ Moxley, Al Selvin, Valerie Sessa, Marydee Spillett, Joan Tavares, Ellen Van Velsor, Michael Wakefield, Martin Wilcox, and John Young.

Cedric Crocker of Jossey-Bass was the person who first encouraged me to write this book. He made it seem possible and inviting. Thanks, Cedric. Also thanks to Byron Schneider and Kathe Sweeney, who guided me through the editorial process. And thanks to Hilary Powers, who did wonderful work copyediting the manuscript.

I am also indebted to colleagues and friends who have supported my work and me personally, who have challenged me to grow, and who have understood me and helped me understand myself better. In addition to everyone already mentioned, these include John Alexander, David DeVries, Barbara Demarest, Joanne Ferguson, Lynn Fick-Cooper, Jill Fields, Bernie Ghiselin, Joan Kofodimos, Mike Lombardo, Ernie Lumsden, Morgan McCall, Carolyn Plumb, John Red, Marian Ruderman, Katie White, all the Card Players (who must remain a secret society), and certainly not least, Laurie Merritt, who provides world-class assistance with New York attitude. You're the best, Laurie.

I would also like to acknowledge all the people—practicing leaders and managers, human resource specialists, organization and leadership development professionals—who have over the last several years listened to me present these ideas. Their points of confusion helped me see where I was unclear myself, their thoughtful questions posed always useful challenges to my way of thinking, and their enthusiasm for what I was trying to say carried me through the difficult moments in writing. I wish I could thank each of you personally.

All of these people, of course, know me mostly in my professional role. My loving wife, Linda, knows me through and through. We have been companions to one another through thirty-four years of marriage. She joins me at the center of who I am. Thank you, Linda, for all you have been and done.

OK, kids, here's your mention in the book. Will, Alice, and Bess, I love you.

# Introduction

Do you feel confused in some way about leadership? When I ask groups of leaders and managers that question, heads nod all over the room. These are people who have heard all the talk about the need for more breadth and depth of leadership. They have heard that leadership should be happening at all levels. That everyone is (or should be) a leader. They have an appreciation for the value of and the need for something like shared leadership to address the increasing complexity of work and to attract and retain the best talent. Yet they feel confused about leadership. I often invite them to talk about this confusion, and as we talk, it soon becomes plain that leadership is confusing because its source is no longer so clear as it once was.

We used to be sure that leadership came from the person in charge. Nowadays, we know that the boss has some kind of responsibility for leadership, but we also hear about empowering followers and making everyone a leader. What does this mean? How can many people be leaders and only one person be responsible? If you make everyone responsible, won't you end up with no one responsible? The more we talk, the less we seem to know.

Why? Why has the idea of leadership become confusing? Isn't leadership, after all, pretty simple? There's a leader and some followers, and the leader leads and the followers follow. What could be plainer than that? What is all the fuss about?

## Leadership in the Twenty-First Century

The central premise of this book is that leadership is in fact changing in ways determined by changes in our way of life, in our ways of understanding, and especially in our ways of interrelating. At the heart of our current confusion about leadership is the persistence of a taken-for-granted idea about leadership that comes to us in a distorted form from the past and from cultures essentially different from our own, an idea that has therefore lost much of its power to make sense to us in our time. I propose that this persistent central idea is that *leadership is something leaders possess as an individual attribute* and, therefore, leadership is given by, created by, leaders. This is the idea of leadership that is causing our confusion.

Obviously such an idea was not confusing in its own time; it was useful and worked well in, say, Edwardian England and in many other contexts that supported the shared understandings and cultural assumptions required to make it work—for example, that leaders were naturally superior, that because of this superiority they took on certain moral duties, and that followers likewise were bound morally to obey someone of greater stature. Given these assumptions, leadership is usefully understood to flow from certain extraordinary personal qualities that set the leader above and before followers. The natural questions asked about leadership then become questions about the personal qualities of leaders; developing leadership becomes a matter of developing leaderlike qualities in individuals.

This way of understanding leadership is not wrong—in fact, it continues to make sense in any number of contexts—but it is limited. We now confront many situations where understanding leadership as the possession of a leader does not make enough sense to make leadership actually work.

Too often in thinking about leadership we are like persons standing on the shore, captivated by the dancing, sparkling whitecaps on the ocean and entirely missing the deep blue sea. The whitecaps are real enough, but their source lies within the action of the ocean itself. This book is therefore not aimed at disproving the idea that leaders create leadership (the whitecaps are accepted as they are). Instead it is an attempt to understand the limitations in this way of understanding leadership and to propose how these limitations can be overcome (how we can look beyond the waves to the deep blue sea), how a new understanding can be forged, and how new possibilities for leadership can be created.

## Relational Leadership

This book provides a framework I will call *relational leadership* that allows us to understand leadership in general in a new way, one designed to help people create and discover new ways of making leadership happen. The existing framework for understanding leadership—the one causing us so much confusion right now—I will call *personal leadership*. In its simplest terms, relational leadership pays attention to the whole system of relations (the deep blue sea) as the creative ground for leadership, while personal leadership pays attention to the character and skill of the leader (the waves and the whitecaps).

*Relational* is not a new word, and I have used many of the ideas of others to build my argument. The fundamental relational idea I take from Kenneth Gergen (1994), who says that individuals are *constituted by their relations*. Robert Kegan (1994) provided another basic idea, which is that adults develop throughout their lifetime by evolving gradually more complex and inclusive frameworks for understanding themselves and the world. I have also used the concept elaborated by Etienne Wenger (1998) that meaning and identity are created when people work together. Along with Nelson Goodman's searching examination of social construction (1978), these ideas form the founding substance of the book you now hold.

In thinking about what I will call relational leadership, I will not assume that individuals are preexisting *entities* already endowed with meaning as such and who then *enter into* relationships. I will thus not assume that there are people who are leaders and others who are followers and that they enter into relationships with one another on the basis of such preexisting qualities. Rather I will assume that individuals are interpenetrating *relationalities* who actually come into being as various kinds of individual persons through connection, interrelation, language, joint action, and the shared creation of knowledge. I will therefore assume that in trying to make leadership happen while working together, people construct one another and *become* such things as leaders and followers.

Do not misunderstand. The uniquely glorious identity of individual persons is not in question here—only the source of that unique identity. The relational idea is not a way of saying that everyone is merely some kind of social clone—far from it. However, the relational idea does propose that individual identities are not self-contained within genes or within the mind as the Western individualist tradition would have it. The relational view is that the glory of our uniqueness comes from our ways of being with others, from our participation in families, groups, communities, and yes, organizations, jobs, task forces, committees. We are who we are, think what we think, love what we love, because of our engagement in creating shared meaning and knowledge with others. This book explores leadership from this relational point of view.

Leadership will be understood not as a possession of the leader but as an aspect of the community (the team, group, organization, association, nation, culture). Leadership will be framed as a communal capacity and a communal achievement. Here is where we will find an approach to building leadership in breadth and depth, to making leadership happen at every level, to seeing how everyone can be a leader. Here is a way to make shared leadership make sense.

This relational framework will encourage us to ask very different questions about leadership: How do people working together in teams, groups, organizations, and communities bring leadership into being? How can their capacity for leadership be increased? What role do individuals play in creating, sustaining, and developing leadership? Is the leader role necessary? The follower role? Are there other roles we have not yet imagined?

## Structure of the Book

The book opens in Chapter One with a discussion of how leadership is called forth by a set of tasks that people who share work need to accomplish—setting direction for the group, creating and maintaining commitment to its purposes, and facing *adaptive challenges*, that is, conditions that require responses that are qualitatively different from past behavior. Getting these leadership tasks taken care of requires that people in a community or organization share some knowledge principle that will allow them to recognize when leadership is happening, when there is in fact a resource present for accomplishing the leadership tasks.

I see three such leadership knowledge principles available for use today: *personal dominance, interpersonal influence,* and *relational dialogue.* Chapter Two presents the personal dominance principle, framing its capacity to make leadership happen and also discussing the ways in which this capacity has become limited. Chapter Three introduces the second principle, interpersonal influence, and attempts to frame just how this principle addresses the limitations of personal dominance and opens up new possibilities for understanding leadership and how it happens.

Chapter Four is a discussion of the contexts and forces that are creating distinct limits to the capacity of interpersonal influence to create effective leadership in our organizations and around the world. Finally, Chapter Five introduces a framing of relational leadership, which I call relational dialogue, a leadership principle addressing the limitations of interpersonal influence and opening up new possibilities for ways of making leadership happen and accomplishing the leadership tasks.

Threaded throughout the book is the story of Zoffner Piano Company, which helps bring the ideas of the book to life, animating what might otherwise be mere abstractions. It is fictional, but is based on my experience over the last ten to fifteen years' work with managers and teams in a variety of organizations large and small, private and public.

What is offered here, then, is a relational way to understand leadership in hopes that it will afford people an approach to constructing a better working version of leadership. It isn't necessary for you to take this idea as your own to read this book usefully—it is enough if you can invite the idea in and entertain it for a while. Later you can ask it to go home, if you please.

Relational leadership does not require that we let go of individuals as leaders. In fact, I hope it will make strong individual leaders more possible again by creating a relational ground on which they can stand. Nor does relational leadership require that we take on the idea that leadership is a search for consensus or collective truth, although I hope it will make new forms of leadership possible, including some that are not dependent on individual leaders. It is, as the book's title suggests, a search for some larger meaning of leadership, a meaning that includes—but is not limited to—the sparkling whitecaps we know as leaders. A meaning that sees how, in making leadership happen, we all swim together in the deep blue sea.

# The Deep Blue Sea

## Chapter One

# Leadership Principles and Leadership Tasks

When her father called her into his office, Elena had a sinking feeling. Her father had not been well in recent years and talked of retiring. Earlier in the day he visited the doctor to get the results of some tests. The tone of his voice on the phone just now was somber. Elena braced herself. She didn't feel ready.

The employees of Zoffner Piano Company referred to Elena's father as Mr. Karl. It was a sign of both their respect for him and their feelings of closeness to him. He knew everything there was to know about making and selling pianos. He was the brains and the heart and the soul of the company. He was also a person who cared about everyone individually, who had countless times come to the rescue of an employee, had provided wise counsel and emotional support. Over the years he tried to instill all of this in Elena, but she knew her father couldn't teach her how to command the attention of everyone on the shop floor when she walked in, or how to help each employee feel important, or how to make the salespeople laugh about a bad quarterly report. These were things that Elena simply couldn't imagine herself doing. Her father was a natural leader, and she was not.

Karl Zoffner had founded Zoffner Piano in 1947 with less than a thousand dollars and a specific idea (what in later years would be called a vision): to build quality pianos that a working person could *afford to buy for a son or daughter. For over fifty years he guided the company through good years and bad by making shrewd decisions about whom to hire, what materials and craftsmanship to use, what markets to go into, where to obtain goods and supplies, which technologies to acquire. Through those years he earned the loyalty and commitment of employees who thought of Zoffner Piano as their second (in some cases, first) family. These people would do anything for Mr. Karl. There were many stories, told and retold, about times when Karl and his employees worked shoulder to shoulder to keep a promise to a customer or to solve a problem with a supplier. When competitors threatened the business, Mr. Karl always found a way to reposition (today we might say reinvent) Zoffner Piano, maintain his original vision, and keep it profitable and growing.*

*Elena came into the business fresh from an MBA program at a leading university. She had not been sure about this decision, and she and her father and mother had spent many a sleepless night discussing her future. In the end she realized that the company was in her blood, even though she was uncertain about her ability to take over from her father. But he insisted that she would learn all she needed to know about the business from helping him run Zoffner Piano until the time came for retirement. Then she would be ready.*

*Karl turned out to be both right and wrong. Elena did learn more than she ever thought she could about the materials that go into a piano, where to get them, how to get the best prices, and about how a piano is made. She learned about casting iron and fashioning wood into piano cases. She learned about marketing the instruments, who buys pianos and why, how much people will pay for a piano for their child, and how much they will pay for a concert instrument. She also began to form some ideas of her own about the company and how she would run it when her father turned it over to her. She looked to him for guidance about leadership, but Karl was not very helpful on that subject.*

*Elena would ask him, "How do you get people to pull together all the time?"*

*He would look a little put out and answer shortly, "I just pull from in front."*

*In fact, her father didn't believe a person could usefully study leadership. "A leader is someone who never thinks about being a leader," he once said. "You just are."*

*This worried Elena. She knew she was not a leader. And that was why she felt uneasy and unprepared walking into her father's office that day.*

## Leadership Principles

If we're lucky, we have known someone like Mr. Karl who just naturally commands attention and respect and who, maybe without ever thinking about it, pulls in the right direction and gets people to follow. Knowing such people can have a lasting effect. Besides providing a model or even a hero to emulate, such people may help convince us that this is the true nature of leadership and that other kinds of leadership we have encountered are only pale imitations offered by people without true leadership ability. As a result we conclude that what we need in this world is more people like Mr. Karl, and that one of the problems we are having in our lives is a lack of true leaders like him. Like Elena, we are often tempted to think that if we can't be a leader like Karl Zoffner, we are not really a leader at all. But how do we come to this conclusion? How do we know that Mr. Karl is the real thing?

## Recognizing Thoughts, Words, and Actions as Leadership

In this book, the question of how we know leadership when we see it plays a central role. I propose that we know leadership when we see it because we share an organizing knowledge principle in common with other people. In other words, Mr. Karl's natural ability to command respect, and our admiration and appreciation of this kind of leadership, come from a way of thinking about leadership, a way of understanding when leadership is happening, that a group of people can share. It is a way of thinking and understanding that enables individuals and the group as a whole to recognize certain thoughts, words, and actions as being leadership.

This alters the usual way to approach the topic of leadership. Usually leadership is assumed to be something out there in the world that exists more or less independent of how we think about it. The way we think about it is mostly determined by the way leadership is. From this more usual point of view, we would think about Mr. Karl's leadership and understand it as being admirable and effective because it *is* admirable and effective. This view is perfectly usable most of the time. It raises the question of what it is about Mr. Karl's leadership that makes it admirable and effective. And that opens up a whole set of considerations as we try to describe and define what it is about Mr. Karl as a person and his approach to leadership that is admirable and effective and perhaps to work out how other people might emulate his approach to leadership.

This book takes the viewpoint that leadership is nothing at all—that even Mr. Karl's leadership doesn't really exist until we have some way of knowing it when we encounter it. If, when encountering certain thoughts, words, or actions, we don't in effect say "that's leadership," then leadership simply isn't what is happening at the moment as far as we are concerned. So in the view being offered here, leadership is not something out there in the world that we come to know because it impresses itself on our minds, it is something we create with our minds by agreeing with other people that *these* thoughts, words, and actions—and not some others—will be known as leadership.

For example, say a young child falls and skins her knee. Her mother runs from the house, sweeps the child in her arms, and with hugs and kisses, comforts the child and takes her into the house to nurse her little wound. Is this an example of leadership? Take a moment to think about this before reading the next paragraph. Try to decide one way or the other.

What was your first response, before you took time to think it over? Did that first response change? What entered into your thinking on this question? How did you come to a conclusion about whether this is an example of leadership or not? If the story had been told to you in some completely different context, would the question of this act being leadership ever have entered your head? How did you deal with the fact that you were being asked to determine if this is an example of leadership or not?

The task I set before you was a way to get at how you may recognize leadership. For some of you, this may have been a rather irritating no-brainer. "Of course that's not leadership, and if this guy thinks it is, I may not read the rest of this book." (Please hang in, however.) Others may have thought it was not leadership at first, but upon reflection, certain aspects of the story, it seemed, might have touched on leadership: the mother is like a leader in that she has a goal in mind (comforting and caring for her child) and she leads the child toward that goal (takes her in her arms, takes her into the house). Or others might have thought it was only minimally like leadership because the mother is caring and concerned, and a leader should be caring and concerned; but otherwise it was not an example of leadership.

All of these ways of answering the question draw on some organizing principle that, in effect, admits certain ideas as being leadership (or possibly being leadership) and blocks other ideas as not being leadership. Thus, if you thought the mother was like a leader because she had a goal in mind and led the child toward that goal, then perhaps you know leadership when there is a person who leads others toward a goal. For you, this would be part of a principle for organizing knowledge of (recognition of) leadership. When you see a person leading others toward a goal, you may recognize that leadership is happening. On the other hand, thoughts, words, and actions that are not recognized as leadership simply cannot be leadership. Maybe nothing in the example seemed remotely close to being leadership. Then leadership was not happening in the story. Only thoughts, words, and actions that are recognized as leadership can constitute leadership.

From this point of view, leadership is not something independent of the way we think. Just the opposite: it is dependent on the way we organize what we take for granted as real and true. The presence or absence of leadership depends on the presence or absence of some knowledge principle that enables a person or a group or a community or organization to say, "That's leadership."

In other words, in this book, we will look at leadership in terms of what makes some thoughts, words, and actions *meaningful as leadership* to people. We will be concentrating on specific ways of knowing and understanding leadership that I believe people share in groups, communities, and organizations. To approach the question of how Mr. Karl manages to make the shop floor fall silent when he passes through, we will address the question of how the people on the shop floor (and Mr. Karl, and we) *come to understand* his very presence as an act of leadership. What are the patterns of ideas and underlying assumptions that cause people to fall silent and that cause us to admire the way Mr. Karl makes people fall silent?

Leadership principles, as these ways of recognizing leadership will be called, are a shared achievement. They are created by people interacting with one another; they are not created in each individual person's mind alone. So there are not as many leadership principles as there are people. And since people interact in many different ways, it is likely that there is not just one master principle from which all other leadership principles are derived. The way of understanding and knowing leadership that brings about Mr. Karl's leadership is just one way to recognize leadership, and there are other ways of understanding and recognizing leadership that are not poor relations to this "real" kind of leadership, but are qualitatively different ways of knowing that leadership is happening. These other ways of understanding leadership bring about thoughts, words, and actions that some people (but not all people) recognize as leadership, but that don't look like Mr. Karl's leadership at all.

To summarize: in this book leadership will be approached as something that is brought into being by a shared knowledge principle that enables people to recognize (know) that leadership is happening. This approach will allow us to talk about leadership as something that can come into being or go out of being because of the presence or absence of some organizing knowledge principle. People share in these knowledge principles as ways of organizing reality about leadership. If they didn't, a group of people would never be able to make leadership happen. So there are not as many principles as people, but there is not just one either. What will be important here is just what such leadership principles are like, how they work or fail to work, what happens when the leadership principle that a group of people has been using becomes less useful to them, and how leadership principles change and evolve.

Later in this chapter I will go into a little more detail about three knowledge principles of leadership. (These are the main topics in later chapters.) But because this talk of principles can be confusing—and because approaching leadership in terms of knowledge principles is such a central idea in this book—it is important to distinguish the idea of leadership principles from two other ideas with which it could be confused, namely, leadership *definitions* and leadership *styles*.

## Principles Distinguished from Definitions

A *knowledge principle* is a set of ideas, a set of rules, if you will, about the nature of reality and life that are taken for granted to be true. Right away, the difference between a knowledge principle and a definition becomes apparent, because most definitions of something as complex as leadership are by their nature subject to debate, doubt, and challenge. Knowledge principles, on the other hand, comprise sets of taken-for-granted truths, truths that are obvious to those who hold them.

For example, when we say something like, "I can't define beauty but I know it when I see it," we are basing our knowledge on some principle by which we recognize and understand beauty. We simply know beauty in this way, without conscious effort. We can recognize and understand beauty when we see it because we apply some knowledge principle of beauty, some set of rules about the nature of reality that implicitly tells us, "It's obvious that this is beautiful." (Of course, different people may use different knowledge principles and thus what is obviously beautiful would be different.) If we were to try to sit down and write a definition of beauty (not recommended) to say what beauty means, the sense of meaning would be afforded by whatever knowledge principle we use to organize what we take to be the reality of beauty. There would be some ideas that we would take for granted as true without question, such as, for example, that natural things—flowers, waterfalls, birds—are beautiful. Thus we might say something like "things in nature are obviously beautiful" and this idea would be part of our beauty principle and would underlie all our thoughts, feelings, responses, and attitudes about beauty. We use knowledge principles all the time, whenever we take it for granted (it is obvious to us) that something is true: nature is beautiful, people are basically good (or bad, or self-interested), God is all powerful, murder is evil.

In the same way, there are leadership principles—principles that allow anyone to say, "I can't define leadership, but I know it when it happens." A leadership principle is thus deeper than a definition of leadership; it is the set of ideas, taken for granted as true, even obvious, that organize and describe the reality behind a definition. To say what leadership means, a definition must make use of some meaning-creating knowledge principle. For example, here is a definition of leadership from F. H. Allport's 1924 *Social Psychology*: "Leadership is personal social control" (cited in Bass, 1990,

p. 12). This definition, like all definitions, is meaningful because it draws on ideas assumed to be true but not dealt with in the definition itself: that a person can exercise social control, that the distinction between what is personal and what is social is useful in leadership, that leadership happens when control happens. If the definition strikes you as being insightful and helps you understand leadership better, if it succeeds in saying what leadership means, it may be because you use the same or a very similar underlying principle for knowing that leadership is happening as the one the definition writer used. Because you share this principle with the writer, the definition helps you articulate something you knew but couldn't put precisely into words. The sharing is critical and makes the definition mean something to you. The definition helps you understand leadership better because it is based on a knowledge principle, a set of taken-for-granted truths, you and the writer share.

If, on the other hand, the definition seems wrong in some way to you, if you respond with "Yes, but—," it may be because you use a different knowledge principle from the one used by the definition writer. You and the writer differ on what you each take to be the reality of leadership. Maybe this definition strikes you as being too narrow; or maybe it seems to describe an outmoded idea of leadership; or maybe it seems to describe power, not leadership. Focusing on the idea of knowledge principles helps us see how these reactions to the definition arise less in an argument over whether it defines leadership effectively and more over differences in taken-for-granted assumptions about reality. That particular definition is a good definition of leadership (it says what the reality of leadership is to you) if, when you see "personal social control" happening in your life, you say "this is leadership." If you don't say that when you see "personal social control" happening, it's not a good definition (it fails to describe what you know the reality of leadership to be).

Here's another definition of leadership, one I think is based on a knowledge principle different from that underlying the definition in the last paragraph: "[Leadership is] a relation between leader and led in which the leader influences more than he is influenced."

(This one is from a 1952 article by H. Gerth and C. W. Mills, "A Sociological Note on Leadership," cited in Bass, 1990, p. 13.) This definition does not even refer to the same ideas as the first. There is no mention of control and no underlying assumption that leadership is personal. Instead, a different way of knowing is being applied: that leadership is interpersonal, a relationship; mutual but unequal influence is what is happening when leadership happens. Assuming that readers of this definition share some of these ways of knowing with the writer of the definition, the definition will make sense to them. In other words, a definition says what leadership means because it makes its assertion within a context of a shared knowledge principle, a sense of what is obviously true that is shared between the definition giver and the definition consumer.

### Principles Distinguished from Styles

So the principles I will present here are not definitions of leadership, although they are the basis of definitions of leadership. They are whole ways of knowing that leadership is happening. This still leaves a question: How is a leadership principle different from a leadership style? It might seem that because differing principles can be expected to bring about differing ways of thinking about leadership, and because differing ways of thinking about leadership could be expected to bring about differing ways of enacting leadership, and given that such differences constitute what we mean by differing leadership styles, it could be argued that a principle and a style are nearly the same. But there is a critical and useful difference between the two. A leadership style is usually thought of as an approach to leadership that a leader (or a follower) chooses to take. A leader chooses to be task-oriented or relationship-focused, or a leader chooses to decide alone or allow followers to participate in a decision. The leader is understood to choose a style depending on the situation, the task, the maturity of the followers, and other considerations. In other words, the idea of style refers to something that a leader can put on or take off, that a leader has control over.

A leadership principle is a different idea. Because a principle is what is required for the leader (and followers!) to recognize that leadership is happening, it is not something you choose to use or not use from one situation to another. Assuming that the leader and the followers want leadership to happen, they are more or less stuck (at least for the present) with whatever leadership principle will allow them to recognize certain thoughts, words, and actions as leadership. This principle will disallow recognition of certain other thoughts, words, and actions as leadership. Without a leadership principle, the people would be unable to recognize any words or actions as leadership—they would be unable to distinguish between what was and was not leadership.

A multitude of differing enactments, approaches, and consciously chosen styles can be understood as leadership from the meaning afforded by a single leadership principle. Likewise, a multitude of enactments, approaches, and styles will not be recognized as leadership, even some that arise from some other leadership principle. Leaders who change their leadership style such that their thoughts, words, and actions are still recognized as leadership are likely still making sense of leadership from the same leadership principle as before. The style has changed, but the principle stays the same. Unlike a leadership style, a leadership principle is changed only slowly and with difficulty, because people don't easily part with a way of making sense of something as important as leadership. As we will discuss later in this book, when a person or a group of people changes their leadership principle, we will view this as the basis for leadership development.

So a leadership principle is deeper than a definition, and is also deeper than a leadership style. A single principle could be used to create definitions of leadership different enough for people to argue over, because people who take the same underlying ideas to be true can still argue over how those taken-for-granted truths apply in life situations. Likewise, a single leadership principle could be the basis for many differing leadership styles. A leadership principle is what gives meaning to definitions and styles in the sense that a principle is required for people to recognize and understand that leadership is what is happening.

## Three Principles for Recognizing Leadership

I have at this point painted myself into a kind of corner. Having proposed the idea of knowledge principles of leadership, I face the task of articulating, spelling out, such principles. The catch-22 in doing this should be obvious after all this discussion of knowledge principles. Whatever articulation of knowledge principles I choose must in itself come from some knowledge principle. Like everyone, I have to take something for granted as true. And what is this knowledge that I myself must take for granted as obviously true? It is the third of the three leadership principles that I will articulate. I cannot see through what I take to be the obvious truths of that principle, and all of my articulation of the first and second principles is based on what I take for granted as being true in the third principle. In this sense, the destination of the whole book is the third principle, and everything else in the book is asserted from the perspective of the understanding of leadership afforded by this third principle.

Having said that, I propose to plunge right in, as if naming and articulating leadership principles were useful and productive. The names I propose for the three leadership principles are *personal dominance* (first principle), *interpersonal influence* (second principle), and *relational dialogue* (the third, and for me, the embedding principle). The following sections will introduce these principles in their basic form. The rest of the book is devoted to a more detailed exploration of the meaning and usefulness of each principle.

### Personal Dominance

Mr. Karl's and his employees' way of recognizing and understanding leadership illustrates an enactment of the first principle: personal dominance. Personal dominance is a way of understanding leadership as the personal quality or characteristic of a certain kind of person called a leader. The particular thoughts, words, and actions of this kind of person can vary along many dimensions without affecting the person's status as a leader because leadership is assumed to come from within, from an inner quality or characteristic, not from this or that behavior. Leadership from this perspective is whatever the (true) leader does: leaders create leadership by expressing an inner quality toward followers.

This principle takes the following truths for granted:

- Leadership is something a person possesses.
- Leadership is an expression of this personally possessed quality or characteristic.
- Leaders lead because followers are convinced of the truth of their leadership.

Dominance does not necessarily mean the same as domination (although it may). *Dominance* refers to the idea that the leader is the source of leadership and the followers are the receivers of leadership. I propose that this is historically the oldest and conceptually the most basic leadership principle.

### Interpersonal Influence

The second leadership principle, interpersonal influence, is a way of understanding that leadership happens when a group of people agree and disagree, ally and contend, concur and argue, plan and negotiate until someone emerges as the most influential person and thus claims the role of leader.

Because this is a different leadership principle from the first principle, I propose that this is a whole different way of creating the meaning of leadership. It is not simply a different approach to leadership that is, say, less power-oriented and less instrumental than the first principle. It is a qualitatively different way to recognize that leadership is happening. The emergence of a leader from a process of negotiation differs from personal dominance because from the perspective of the second principle a person becomes a leader by achieving influence, whereas in the first principle a person is the leader by possessing the quality or characteristic of leadership. In the first principle, leadership is in the leader; in the second principle, leadership is in the greater influence created by the process of negotiation. In the first principle, influence is one of many tools the leader possesses as an aspect of personal leadership. In the second principle, influence must be achieved, and in its achievement, one takes on leadership.

This principle takes the following truths for granted:

- Leadership is a role occupied by the most influential person.
- People possess or can acquire certain qualities and characteristics that enable them to be effective in such a role.
- Leadership involves followers actively in the process of negotiating influence.
- Leaders lead by influencing followers more than followers influence them.

I propose that this second principle comes into being because of certain limitations of the first principle, and that historically it arose in human life later than the first principle and as a response to these limitations.

### Relational Dialogue

The third leadership principle, relational dialogue, is a way of understanding that leadership happens when people who acknowledge shared work use dialogue and collaborative learning to create contexts in which that work can be accomplished across the dividing lines of differing perspectives, values, beliefs, cultures, and more generally what I will refer to as differing worldviews. Again, this is yet another qualitatively different way to recognize that leadership is happening.

This principle takes the following truths for granted:

- Leadership is the property of a social system.
- Individual people do not possess leadership; leadership happens when people participate in collaborative forms of thought and action.
- If there is an individual leader, the actions that person takes are an aspect of participation in the process of leadership.

This third principle may strike the ear strangely. It is less familiar than the first two principles, I propose, because it has just begun to emerge and is not yet fully formed. It is emerging, however, in response to certain limitations in the second principle that are calling this third principle forth, and people in communities and organizations are already beginning to make sense of leadership in this way.

With the idea of leadership principles in mind, and remembering that we will be visiting each of the three principles later in detail, let's return to the story of Elena Zoffner, her father, and the Zoffner Piano Company.

*In Karl Zoffner's office that day, Elena received the news that she was the new head of the company. Her father was stoical, as always, but she could tell it was a profoundly sad day for him. Her own feelings were more complex: a combination of sadness and excitement, a sense of something lost and something just on the verge of coming into being. That very day she overheard a long-time employee talking to a younger worker. The announcement of Mr. Karl's retirement and her taking over had just been made.*

*"The girl is a good kid, but she knows nothing. I tell you, with-out Mr. Karl we're in big trouble."*

Elena was long past letting this kind of remark bother her too much. And anyway she agreed that her knowledge of the business could never equal her father's. The remark did, however, drive home to her that somehow she had to get out from under her father's shadow as soon as possible. As long as she was compared to her father, she would always be found wanting in the eyes of the employees. So she struck out to make an impression on people in her own right. She figured that she needed to take the company in a new direction, one that her father would never have contemplated. Elena decided that Zoffner Piano would get into the business of making di-gital pianos.

The reaction at the weekly management meeting when Elena made this intention clear was one of stony silence. Her words were greeted with a variety of hard looks ranging from puzzlement to dis-may to outrage. No one dared to say a word. They simply stared at Elena, seemingly embarrassed for her.

*"Of course we will continue to make the same fine pianos we always have. We'll add the digital piano to our line of products. This will mean opening a new plant and hiring more employees. It's a whole new direction for us, and I'm very excited about it."*

They shifted in their seats uncomfortably. No one spoke.

*"It's the future."* Elena continued, feeling somehow more confi-dent in herself despite them. *"Digital instruments are growing in pop-ularity. It's an enormous opportunity for us to grow."*

John, the marketing manager, found his voice. *"So you want me to do some research on this, Elena? I could study the digital market and find out how well positioned we would be to enter it."*

*"You do your study, John, but the decision is made. This is where Zoffner is headed. I take full responsibility for this. It's my call."*

*"Of course it's your call, Elena. I was just thinking that we might want to look first before we, you know, before we leap."*

*"Too late, John, we have already leaped."*

*The next day, unknown to Elena, the head foundryman, an old-world craftsman responsible for casting the iron pin boards, went to see Karl.*

*"So now we are going to make toy pianos, Mr. Karl?"*

*Karl was surprised by Elena's decision and by the foundryman's visit. He had expected that Elena might take Zoffner in some new directions, but not this. He believed making digital pianos would lower the value of the Zoffner piano in the eyes of the customer, and they would not be able to maintain their margins. He had discussed this with his daughter several times in the past. He was filled with doubt about her decision and what to do about it, but he knew exactly what to say now.*

*"This is Elena's decision, Anthony. She's in charge now."*

*"But Mr. Karl! What will become of us? What will happen to us when people see that we make these things?"*

*"You know that's not your concern, and frankly I'm surprised at you, Anthony. You never questioned one of my decisions like this. What has gotten into you?"*

*"I'm sorry, Mr. Karl. Very, very sorry."*

*When word got around that Anthony had quit because of Elena's decision, morale at Zoffner fell. Employees grumbled among themselves and the rumor mill started working overtime. "Mr. Karl is coming back" was, of course, the leading rumor. Karl took Elena aside and tried to get her to change her mind, but Elena was ready for this. She reminded Karl of his own words. "You said it was mine now, Father. These are my decisions now, just like they were your decisions in the past. Don't expect me to be you. I've got to be myself." For all his doubt about her business judgment, Karl felt utterly proud of his daughter at that moment.*

*The employees were not so easy to deal with. They became increasingly distrustful of Elena, and their poor attitude began to show up in production problems and absenteeism. For the first time in the company's history, turnover was becoming a problem. Elena saw that people were not committed to their work the way they had once been. The new people hired to replace those that left seemed to want no more out of a job than their paycheck. To Elena, they had no pride in their work. She became obsessed with maintaining the quality of their product and instituted a number of work procedures and rules to ensure quality that had never been needed in her father's day. The world was changing, and so was Zoffner Piano.*

## Leadership Tasks

We discussed the idea that for certain thoughts, words, and actions to be recognized, understood, and known as leadership, people in a community or organization must share some knowledge principle that allows them to agree that leadership is happening. But no matter what leadership principle is used to recognize leadership, the call for leadership arises in the need to accomplish certain tasks.

### The Work of Leadership: Direction, Commitment, Adaptation

The tasks of leadership will be articulated here as setting direction, creating and maintaining commitment, and facing adaptive challenge. It is the need to accomplish these tasks that calls forth leadership based on whatever principle people in the community or organization hold in common.

Notice that these are the very tasks that the people at Zoffner Piano are having a hard time accomplishing since Mr. Karl's retirement: the direction of the company is unclear, a matter of doubt and debate; people are not committed to the company or to Elena; and they are facing a challenge (the retirement of Mr. Karl and the move to digital keyboards) to which they are having a great deal of trouble adapting. When the leadership tasks of a community or organization are not being accomplished, people in the organization or community will say that they lack leadership. Exactly what thoughts, words, and actions constitute leadership, and what they therefore see themselves as lacking, depends on the leadership principle they share in common and use to know when leadership is (and therefore when it is not) happening.

The three leadership tasks as expressed here—setting direction, creating commitment, and facing adaptive challenges—are intended to be merely representative of a broad range of leadership tasks, which could be articulated in many different ways—defining mission, setting goals, creating vision, motivating followers, forging community, creating alignment, creating change, managing change, fostering innovation, and so forth. Leadership tasks seem to center on three kinds of tasks related to direction (mission, goals, vision, purpose), commitment (alignment, motivation, spirit, teamwork), and adaptation (innovation, change, dealing with paradigm shifts). Thus we will simplify by working with the three leadership tasks of setting direction, creating commitment, and facing adaptive challenges as if these three were an adequate representation of leadership tasks in general.

First let's take a closer look at each of these critical leadership tasks, and then we will look ahead briefly to a main topic of this book: how each leadership principle approaches the accomplishment of these tasks.

***Setting Direction.*** The task of setting direction answers some basic questions: Where are we going? What are we going to do?

Why are we doing it? What purpose will we serve? What will we become and do in the future? How will we get there? These are all questions of direction that people ask one another in some form all the time, whether it's a small group of friends planning an evening together or a huge multinational corporation devising a long-term strategy. Direction as a leadership task is related both to the destination and the path toward the destination. It involves the articulation of mission, vision, purpose, values; the naming of goals, outcomes, criteria of effectiveness; the devising of strategies, tactics, modes, methods. Direction tells people what they are doing, why they are doing it, and how they will do it. In a small group of friends going out for the evening, the question of direction can be answered quickly and easily because the question of what to do usually implies and answers the questions of why and how. But in contexts such as a large community or organization, direction becomes more complex. Answering the question of what to do can leave unanswered the questions of why and how; people can agree on what and disagree on why and how. This complexity argues for breaking out the various aspects of direction in thinking about leadership, and usually this is what happens. Considerations of mission and vision are separated from considerations of strategy and effectiveness. For simplicity in trying to understand the idea of leadership principles, however, the leadership tasks will be presented here in a generalized form.

***Creating and Maintaining Commitment.*** The second task of leadership is creating and maintaining commitment. How can a group, community, or organization stay together, work together, cooperate, become aligned and coordinated? How will everyone pull together in the same direction when things get tough, when some degree of self-sacrifice is required? How can people in a group or community or organization know that they can count on one another? Commitment is related to cohesion, coordination, and investment. It involves creating the tie that binds, the organizational glue, the sense of togetherness. It also involves what many thoughtful people prefer to think of as a management function rather than a leadership task: coordination and alignment. (I propose that what we think of as management has its own knowledge principles that are more or less independent of leadership principles, and yet much of the work of management and leadership overlap. Hence the confusion between management and leadership: the two are aspects of overlapping work that must be accomplished according to more or less independent working principles.) The leadership task of coordination and alignment has to do with creating a context in which people will allow themselves to be in the service of the plans and needs of others. (The management aspect of this task deals more with the technical aspects of structuring coordination and alignment.) Finally, creating commitment involves maintaining commitment, that is, keeping people together and aligned when forces arise that would pull them apart.

*Facing Adaptive Challenge.*   The third leadership task is facing adaptive challenge. The phrase *adaptive challenge* here is being used in the sense that Ron Heifetz uses it: a challenge confronting a community or organization for which it has no preexisting resources, remedies, tools, solutions, or even the means for accurately naming and describing the challenge. Thus most challenges are not adaptive, they are merely problems or decisions needing to be made. Everyday problems present situations for which the community or organization is prepared, or for which it has the means to get prepared. Such everyday problems might require a high degree of creativity and resourcefulness and may be quite difficult to solve, but they are fundamentally approachable using means that are already available or can be marshaled. Solving such everyday problems is not taken here to be a leadership task. Making such everyday decisions is not what is meant here by facing adaptive challenges. An adaptive challenge causes confusion. Its challenge is precisely this: that people in the community or organization cannot agree on the nature of the challenge, the degree of its significance, or sometimes whether a challenge exists or not. The organization has no tools for approaching an adaptive challenge because it has no widespread, agreed-on understanding of the challenge. Differing ways of understanding the challenge are being offered and each differing understanding implies different responses. To face an adaptive challenge the group or organization must first create a shared sense of what it is and what it means before people can begin to create the resources for responding. Facing an adaptive challenge will therefore fundamentally change the community or organization.

All three leadership tasks are framed as being related to the very existence of a group, community, or organization. Setting direction can and often does bring a community or organization into being; losing direction or failing to set direction can mean losing meaning and the very reason for being. Creating and maintaining commitment sustains the community or organization and enables people to serve their own needs and the needs of others. When this task is not accomplished, the community or organization can literally fall apart—the most inspiring direction cannot hold it together because, without commitment, there is no way to reach the destination. Facing adaptive challenges is critical to the long-term viability of a community or organization. Failing to accomplish this task can mean that the context in which a community or organization has set direction and created commitment changes such that the direction and the basis for commitment are nullified. Even in accomplishing this task, a community or organization faces fundamental change that may significantly alter the identity of the community—and this new identity might imply the loss of the community that once was.

## How Each Principle Approaches the Leadership Tasks

Thus these three leadership tasks can be articulated in a general sense. But, as I hope is becoming clear, such leadership tasks are not likely to be understood in the same way from the perspective of each of the principles outlined earlier. The interpretation and understanding of each of the tasks will differ depending on the principle, as does the interpretation and understanding of leadership itself. This creates a distinctive capacity and limitation for each leadership principle with respect to accomplishing the leadership tasks. A brief overview of the way each leadership principle approaches the accomplishment of the leadership tasks will be helpful before we move on to a closer examination of the leadership principles themselves.

***Personal Dominance.*** The first leadership principle makes sense of direction as the clear and univocal expression of the leader's vision. As an extension of an ability that is understood to be personally possessed by the leader, direction is the leader's personal, and therefore unified, vision. In a community or organization that understands leadership from the perspective of the first principle and possesses an effective dominant leader, direction is synonymous with leadership because both direction and leadership flow from the leader. The discourse of this principle is that of personality, belief in personal power, the language of character, vision, and inspiration. As we will see, this capacity of the first principle to create clear direction can also put limitations on its efficacy in some contexts. When the leader's personal direction proves to be less than effective, the basis of leadership itself is undermined.

Followers commit directly and personally to the leader—not just because of their belief in the efficacy or rightness of the leader's vision but because of their belief in the leader's being as a leader. Mr. Karl was able to create powerful commitment and keep it over a long period because the employees of Zoffner Piano believed in him personally as their natural and inevitable leader. Followers who understand leadership from the perspective of the first principle commit to what they sense as the inner quality, the personal strength, and the integrity of character of the leader. This can forge a powerful bond between leader and followers, but, again, it can also pose a critical limitation—loss of commitment to the leader personally, for whatever reason, severely undermines leadership itself.

Because an adaptive challenge is understood here as one requiring a fundamental change in understanding, a shift in values, a sea change in direction that faces the whole community or organization, such a challenge is unlikely to be recognized as a leadership task from the perspective of the first principle. To the extent that an adaptive challenge is not recognizable and interpretable in terms the leader already understands, an adaptive challenge is more likely to be understood as a cataclysm, an event or circumstance beyond the control of the leader and thus of the community or organization. The community or organization as a whole will therefore lack the capacity not only to accomplish this task but even to understand it as a leadership task.

***Interpersonal Influence.*** Direction is understood and approached from the perspective afforded by the second principle as a negotiated outcome, a vector of differing perspectives resolved in the vision of the leader—the person who emerges as having the most influence. This is a marked departure from the way the first principle makes sense of direction. The inclusion of perspectives outside of the leader's means that direction is no longer univocal, a single voice speaking from a single worldview. Instead, the voice is that of a leader who has taken account of other perspectives in articulating a perspective for the group. There is still a unity in the direction, but it is a unity composed of the convergence of parts, the relativizing of differing perspectives into a whole. The discourse of science and engineering is strongly invoked from the perspective of the second principle—direction is a theory of how multiple perspectives can be unified by an overarching perspective.

Commitment is created in the second principle through the negotiation of influence. Participating in this process binds its participants to one another because each person stands to gain (although in practice not everyone does, of course) a double payoff—personal fulfillment and communal or organizational fulfillment. The second principle makes sense of commitment by enlisting the self-interest of individuals and linking it to the accomplishment of collective work. Commitment from the perspective of the second principle is not follower to leader only, but also leader to follower and follower to follower.

The capacity to frame an adaptive challenge—a challenge requiring fundamental transformations in the community or organization—as a task that can be accomplished by leadership is perhaps the key achievement of the second principle. Such transformation of a community or organization becomes at least possible from the perspective of the second principle. Influence can, after all, be renegotiated, new patterns of understanding and new leaders can emerge. However, as we will see in later chapters, it is in attempting to accomplish this task in the face of unresolvable difference that the second principle encounters a key limitation.

*Relational Dialogue.*   The third principle recognizes leadership as an embracing of differences, an openness to the continuous unfolding of possibility. Direction is therefore multivalent and holds differences without resolving them. It is radically open to multiple interpretations and evaluations and derives its efficacy from this very openness. Such direction comprises ambiguity, uncertainty, and multiple meanings. This requires movement away from the second principle's reliance on the convergent discourses of science and engineering and toward the realm of art, where divergent, ambiguous multiple meanings can be crafted into a sensible, though unresolved, whole. Setting direction is accomplished through shared exploration of deliberately polysemous tools such as narrative, symbol, picture, and metaphor.

Commitment is created and maintained through participation in the shared creation of an unknown future. Whereas in the second principle people commit to one another in the expectation of some personal and communal benefit that is more or less spelled out, in the third principle people commit to the process of crafting a future in which individuals have no way of knowing what the personal outcome will be. Commitment is to transformation toward an unknown future. Letting go of the self, seeking a completion of the self in an unknown-but-shared future shapes commitment in the third principle. This may seem unlikely at first and against simple reason with respect to a person's presumed self-interest. But remember that people commit to such unknown potentiality all the time, when they explore and invent, when they innovate and invest, when they fall in love and marry, bear and raise children. We have not in the past seen these forms of commitment as aspects of accomplishing a leadership task. From the perspective of the third principle, they become recognized as such.

Because the third principle recognizes leadership as the crafting of a sensible but unresolved whole out of differing and even conflicting worldviews, its capacity for flexibility of understanding in the face of an adaptive challenge is great. A wide range of possible interpretations and evaluations of worldviews and paradigms is available to the community or organization, coupled with modes of discourse that do not privilege one worldview above another but seek ways forward while holding difference. From the perspective of the third principle, accomplishing the leadership task of facing an adaptive challenge is an ongoing feature of leadership.

## Conclusion

I propose that something like these three leadership principles (along with the related ways of interpreting and approaching the leadership tasks) constitutes the totality of what we think of as leadership in any complex community or organization. I propose that a systemic view of leadership, that is, a view of leadership as the property of a social system, is most usefully framed not in terms of a single and ultimately unified phenomenon (social influence, for example), no matter the degree of complexity in that framing, but in terms of distinctly and qualitatively differing shared meaning-making principles.

Table 1.1 summarizes this totality of leadership in terms of the three principles and the three leadership tasks as I have articulated them.

**Table 1.1  Summary of Leadership
Principles and Leadership Tasks**

| Tasks \ Principles | 1. Personal Dominance | 2. Interpersonal Influence | 3. Relational Dialogue |
|---|---|---|---|
| Setting direction | Unified, clear direction that is based in the worldview of the leader. | Direction is based on a negotiation of differences integrated in the leader's perspective. | Direction holds differences and is multivalent. |
| Creating commitment | Commitment is to the leader personally. | Commitment is to the leader's integrating vision. | Commitment is to the shared crafting of possibilities. |
| Facing adaptive challenge | An adaptive challenge can be faced to the extent that the leader is predisposed. | An adaptive challenge can be faced through a renegotiation of influence. | An adaptive challenge can be faced through dialogue across worldviews. |

I hope this brief preview of the ideas presented in this book has invited your curiosity and interest. To repeat, the hypothesis is this: particular thoughts and actions become "leadership" and accomplish leadership tasks because of some underlying and organizing knowledge principle, usually unconsciously held, that affords people a sense that those particular words and actions "simply are" leadership—"I can't define it, but I know it when I see it." Different people in a community or organization may understand and recognize leadership from differing perspectives afforded by different leadership principles. These people will tend to disagree with one another not simply on the effectiveness of certain thoughts and actions as leadership, but on the point of whether those thoughts and actions constitute leadership at all. They speak different languages of leadership, in effect. This has critical implications for the accomplishment of the leadership tasks. If there are people who, because of the principle from which they view certain thoughts and actions, do not see leadership happening, then for them the leadership tasks cannot be accomplished—for them direction cannot be set, they cannot become committed, they cannot face an adaptive challenge. The purpose of this book is to articulate leadership principles in hopes of helping people in communities and organizations learn to create meaning and accomplish leadership tasks across, not just within, these knowledge principles. The last chapter deals with this question of simultaneously "holding" all three leadership principles within a single community or organization.

A couple of disclaimers are in order here. First, the leadership principles are not intended in and of themselves to be recipes for effective leadership. As I hope is becoming clear, leadership effectiveness is related more to the sharing of meaning in a community than it is to any particular style or approach to leadership. Thus leadership effectiveness is a matter of developing shared discourses—shared ways of understanding how the leadership tasks can be accomplished—and is not primarily a matter of getting leaders to display certain attitudes or act in certain ways.

When I'm talking with people about these ideas, they often ask me, What does the third principle look like? How would we do this? My answer is invariably unsatisfying, and for good reason: I don't know. But neither do I know with certainty what the first principle looks like, if we take this to mean that certain words and actions definitely reflect meanings as constructed in the first principle. This is something we can never be sure about based on a view from outside a community. Only by entering into the community and inquiring into the shared meaning-making languages and processes of the community can we find the principle. Principles in practice can take many different forms. I suspect there are forms of the first principle that might look like consensus and total involvement of followers by the leader; likewise there may turn out to be forms of the third principle that look like a dominant leader taking charge. Such forms are not, at any rate, ruled out by the idea of leadership-constituting principles.

Second, I am not claiming that the leadership principles as I articulate them are empirically verifiable as the real and true principles of leadership, or as the only way to articulate leadership principles. This expression of principles is based in my experience of talking to managers and executives in organizations about leadership and leadership development, and my reading about the theory of leadership, its practice and development. Inevitably, then, it is my way of understanding that gives voice to these leadership principles. On the other hand, I do not believe that my way of understanding or my voice is unique or idiosyncratic. My understanding emerges from my participation in a reality that is the co-creation of many people who enact leadership, develop leadership, and think and write about leadership.

Finally, I am not claiming that leadership principles are capable of being expressed universally to all people at all times—in fact, I am pretty sure they are not. It would be interesting for someone from another culture to try to articulate leadership principles in that context. Would we learn that such principles would not cause us in our culture to recognize leadership at all? Or would we find similarities and parallels in how leadership is recognized in differing cultures?

Looking at the plight of Elena and the people of Zoffner Piano Company in terms of leadership knowledge principles, I suggest that one of the things happening at this moment in their history is that a new principle of leadership is being called forth. Mr. Karl and the employees for many years made sense of leadership from the perspective of the first principle. Elena's feeling that she "is not a leader" in the same sense as her father initiates her growing recognition that some different principle of leadership will be required to accomplish the leadership tasks at Zoffner. We will be following along as she and the employees of the company develop what is for them a new way to understand leadership, a new principle. As we will see later on, this is what I am proposing is the foundation for leadership development at a systemic level in a community or organization: the emergence of a new leadership principle in response to encountering limits of an existing principle, followed by the integration of existing and new principles. But before we go down that path, let's look more deeply at the principle that Zoffner Piano used to accomplish leadership with such great effect for so many years: the personal dominance principle.

## Chapter Two

# Personal Dominance

What was the essence of leadership at Zoffner Piano Company for all those years under Mr. Karl? What is it that Elena now believes she lacks and that the employees don't see in her? Why is there a leadership crisis, a lack of leadership, now that Elena has taken over from her father? The first leadership principle provides an answer to these kinds of questions: the essence of leadership is a quality that belongs to Mr. Karl himself. Whether by birth or development, Mr. Karl is a leader. He possesses leadership ability as a matter of his character, personality, and psychology. What Elena lacks is just this same inner quality of leadership. Whether by birth or lack of development, she does not possess leadership ability, or enough leadership ability, just as the average person does not possess the athletic ability of Michael Jordan.

The employees of Zoffner Piano see this lack in her as plainly as they see the presence of leadership ability in her father. They are worried about the company and have a sense of being on a ship adrift without a rudder. Where will direction come from? How will they regain their sense of commitment? How will they adapt to change? Elena herself sees the situation in the same way. She knows she is not a leader like her father. She and the employees share a sense of leadership crisis now that her father has retired.

This way that Elena and the employees have of understanding the situation at Zoffner is a shared worldview. Elena's own doubts about her leadership ability tend to become confirmed by the pessimism of the employees, while their pessimism is partly rooted in her self-doubt. It is the reverse of the situation under Mr. Karl, when his self-confidence and the employees' optimism mirrored one another. This kind of reciprocity in making sense of a situation is what I mean when I speak of a shared knowledge principle, a shared way of understanding when leadership is or is not happening. In the case of Zoffner Piano, it is the same knowledge principle for understanding leadership that underlies both the effective leadership of Mr. Karl and the ineffective leadership of Elena: the personal dominance principle. It is by virtue of sharing this leadership principle that Mr. Karl and Elena and all the employees at Zoffner know that leadership is missing now that Mr. Karl has retired. It is not something they are deluded about. Leadership really is missing, because the knowledge principle they use to tell them when leadership is happening is telling them it is not happening with Elena in charge.

## The Meaning of Personal Dominance

Let's take some time to look more closely at the meaning of personal dominance as a shared knowledge principle for understanding leadership. Remember that such a principle organizes a set of taken-for-granted truths that people use to recognize leadership when it happens—or when it fails to happen. (When I say the truths are taken for granted I do not mean to imply that they are in some way not true, that people are "taking" them to be true when they are in fact false. I mean that these ideas are for the most part not questioned and are usually not even considered *to be questionable* by people who use them to make sense of their experience of leadership.) What then do I propose are these taken-for-granted truths of the personal dominance principle?

### Dominance Is Natural

As a matter of natural variation, some people are predisposed to be dominant in relation to others. This truth would seem to be fundamental to the first principle. Though one might deplore the facts of dominance from an ethical perspective, it is taken for granted that people who are physically strong tend to rule people who are weak, that people who are fast tend to get ahead of people who are slow. Such physical facts lend themselves to other inferences about dominance, such as that people who are courageous tend to win out over people who are cowardly, that people who are inventive tend to outsmart people who are conventional, or that people who are confident and self-assured will naturally best people who are uncertain and timid.

Our first experience of this truth comes as children in relation to our parents. A first understanding of leadership—for those of us fortunate enough to have been blessed with concerned and attentive parents—probably comes from seeing how a mother or father, strong, capable, and seemingly all-knowing, would set direction, lay down the rules, reward us when we were good, and punish us when we did wrong. We were committed to our parents as surely as we could ever be to anyone. If we were among the lucky ones, the challenges and problems of life floated over our heads unnoticed.

As we grow up we have experiences over and over that tend to confirm this truth. Even as we begin to see through the dominance of parents, we meet others who take their place as dominant figures: teachers, pastors, friends, mentors, bosses. We may also, of course, come to count ourselves as being among those who are stronger, smarter, more resourceful.

## Dominant People Are Natural Leaders

Imagine a group of humans tens of thousands of years ago about to set out on a journey into unknown territory. For such a band of people to be successful, to reach their destination, stay together, and overcome the obstacles and dangers along the way, they will need someone to go first, to literally lead the way. Everyone in this band will have someone in front to follow except for the leader. Such a person had better be strong, cunning, inventive, resourceful. This person must face danger before anyone else, must make decisions about which obstacles to face and which to avoid, must be able to marshal whatever is at hand to overcome challenges, many of which cannot be anticipated at the beginning of the journey. And in case the band meets with opposition, the person going first had better be able to intimidate or defeat an enemy. Such a leader must also be able to master the fears and doubts of followers; literally keep them in line and make sure they remain loyal. Clearly a dominant person, standing figuratively and perhaps literally above the others, is best suited to be first in line, to be the leader.

It is not far from the facts of this kind of scenario to the conclusion that it is the *nature* of dominant people to lead, that being dominant and being a leader are really the same thing. It follows from this that when a leader is required, a dominant person is required.

## Leadership Is Personal

Leadership, then, is taken as being obviously personal, the personal possession of a dominant person. It originates in the leader, is a product of the leader, is the leader's gift to followers. It is an aspect of the person's individual being, an aspect of personality, character, psychology. The nature of leadership is identical with the nature of the leader. If the leader is harsh, demanding, unyielding, this will be the nature of leadership. If the leader is kind, caring, forgiving, leadership will be the same.

Developing leadership, then, becomes a matter of identifying people who are natural leaders and getting them into the right positions where they can express their leadership for the benefit of the community or organization. The emphasis many organizations put on selection and succession planning may be understood as an enactment of the personal dominance principle.

## Leadership Happens When a Leader Expresses Leadership Toward Followers

Leadership is brought into being when a leader expresses this inner quality toward followers. Leadership is lost when the leader is lost or when the leader stops expressing leadership. Although followers may have many differing kinds of effects on the leader, leadership itself is essentially a one-way flow of what is within the leader toward the followers, directing, inspiring, motivating, evaluating, rewarding, and punishing.

Leadership, then, is what the leader does. The leader's actions are leadership, whether good leadership or bad. If we are interested in understanding leadership, we will find such natural leaders and observe their behavior; this will inform us about the nature of leadership—both good and bad, effective and ineffective. But that nature will be found to be highly variable, and generalizing about the traits of leaders will produce long lists of possible qualities. In general, such lists will boil down to qualities of dominance.

## The Leader's Job Is to Accomplish the Leadership Tasks

Setting direction, creating and maintaining commitment, and facing adaptive challenges are tasks the leader accomplishes on behalf of the community. The ability to accomplish these tasks for the benefit of the community or organization distinguishes effective from ineffective leadership. If the leader is effective in accomplishing the tasks, the community or organization moves in accordance with the leader's vision, aligns with the leader's plans, responds to the leader's call, adapts as the leader adapts. If the leader fails to accomplish the tasks, the community or organization drifts aimlessly, loses a sense of purpose, falls apart, stops making sense as a community.

At Zoffner Piano, Mr. Karl had the personal knowledge of the piano, how to manufacture pianos, how to market and sell them, how to run a business that makes pianos. He had the personality to command attention and to form relationships with people of all kinds who worked for him. He used these personal qualities to set direction; people committed to him because they trusted him personally; he faced the problems of the business personally and solved them personally.

### Followers Depend on the Leader

Because the leader accomplishes the leadership tasks on behalf of the community, followers depend on the leader not just for direction, commitment, and adaptation, but more widely for their sense of meaning and belonging. The meaningfulness of their work in the community is highly dependent on the extent to which the leader accomplishes the leadership tasks. Followers obey and commit to the leader because the leader shows the way toward some purpose or mission that gives meaning. Not to obey and commit to the leader risks being left behind, facing one's fate alone, losing one's place of belonging in the community. Most important, not to obey risks losing significance.

## Shading the Meaning of Personal Dominance

I have tried to give a sense of the personal dominance principle as an organization of taken-for-granted truths. In doing so, for the sake of emphasis and clarity, I have probably overdrawn the portrait. In the next section I will try to soften and add complexity to this picture.

For example, natural physical dominance is hardly ever the basis for leadership in today's communities and organizations. The picture of the strong and brave leader going first into the unknown is surely overdrawn. More often, dominance is assumed in other attributes, many of which can be found on some lists of leadership competencies: intelligence, resourcefulness, creativity, integrity, passion, trustworthiness, empathy. It is not the attributes themselves that are the issue here. Rather, it is the understanding of them as traits that leaders possess as a matter of their personal makeup and that they have in abundance over followers that arises from the perspective provided by the personal dominance principle.

The whole idea that leadership happens when the leader acts, that followers depend on the leader to accomplish the leadership tasks, may strike a distinctly paternalistic chord—or worse, may smack of coercion and manipulation, the strong lording it over the weak. On the other hand, to see the actions of a dominant leader and the dependence on such a leader as aspects of paternalism or coercion is to *lose* the sense of leadership provided from the perspective of the first principle. This interpretation of dominant leadership misses the point, as it were, and fails to appreciate the power of personal dominance to provide meaning by questioning the truth of its basic assumptions. Leadership can happen only to the extent that the knowledge principle by which it is understood is taken to be true knowledge.

This may all seem to be some version of a long-lost kind of leadership: heroic leadership. This principle of leadership is constantly invoked in conversations about great men and women who have accomplished extraordinary things. We can hardly talk about such people without invoking dominance to make sense of how they accomplished what they did. Whether or not the personal dominance principle provided the meaning of leadership for Gandhi and his followers, for example, or for Carrie Nation and the members of the Women's Christian Temperance Union whom she inspired, we invoke personal dominance in retrospect to understand how leadership happened.

Even when people think of a Fortune 500 company's needing leadership in the person of a dynamic CEO, the dominance principle is being invoked—at least in thinking about who is needed, if not in actual practice in the corporation. Even though the situation in such an organization is by no means a case of people "going in a line into the unknown," the dominance principle underlies the idea that the person of the CEO will bring the intelligence, power, strength (perhaps of character), and resourcefulness to marshal the organization, forge clear direction, gain commitment, and face challenges. The dominance principle underlies the idea that leadership is inherent in the person of the CEO, that the quality of leadership will be directly related to the personal qualities of the CEO.

In some ways, the understanding of leadership afforded by the personal dominance principle frames the whole idea of good leadership in our culture: a dominant leader articulating a clear and compelling vision that inspires followers, generates extraordinary effort and loyalty, and overcomes challenges and obstacles. Instead of being an outmoded and hopelessly romantic, heroic version of leadership, I propose that this first principle is still very much in daily use in communities and organizations to make sense of leadership.

## The First Principle and the Leadership Tasks

Let's try to get a better sense of leadership as understood from the perspective of the personal dominance principle by examining how people invoking leadership based on this principle would go about accomplishing the leadership tasks. It is important here to try to understand the achievement of this principle with respect to our human need to accomplish these tasks. In doing this, I will try to avoid two extremes—neither on one hand treating the first principle as "true" leadership, in comparison with which other ways of understanding leadership are pale reflections, nor on the other hand treating the first principle as an outmoded heroic form of leadership that should be firmly relegated to the past. The point here is to understand and appreciate the way of thinking about leadership that is possibly at the heart of all thinking about leadership. If it is true, as has been claimed, that humans survive through cooperation (that cooperation is our "ecological niche"), then the leadership tasks as a critical element in framing such cooperation and the first leadership principle as a way to understand accomplishing those tasks represent critical achievements in human thought.

## Setting Direction

From the perspective on leadership afforded by the personal dominance principle, followers look directly to the leader for direction.
At first, and especially for those who do not make sense of leadership from this perspective, this may seem to be a hopeless kind of
dependence and an almost childlike faith in the power of the
leader. Remember, however, that from the logic of this principle,
the leader is understood to possess as a personal quality just those
aspects of character and knowledge that people in the community
or organization most admire, or most respect, or (in some cases)
most fear. This is why followers who understand leadership from
the first principle look to the leader for direction; the leader, being
the exemplar of what is right, good, powerful, intelligent, is naturally the best person to provide direction and to know what needs
to be done. Knowing what needs to be done does not mean simply
doing whatever it might occur to the leader to do; it means knowing what makes sense to the community, what the needs and desires
of the community are, what will work in the context of the community. The possession of this kind of knowledge is integral to the
possession of leadership ability. A person lacking this kind of knowledge would be necessarily understood to lack leadership ability.

Think about the growth and success of Zoffner Piano Company
under the leadership of Karl Zoffner. He set the direction from the
first by articulating the company's strategy—his strategy—for the
company. Key factors in any craftsperson's decision to join the company and to stay would have been Mr. Karl's character, his personal
quality, his knowledge of making pianos, his ability to execute the
strategy. No skilled person would have put up with an amateur in
this regard (as Elena is discovering). The leader of the company
had better be an example to others and know as much or more
than any of the craftspeople about their business. In addition to a
knowledge of each individual craft going into the construction of
a piano, Mr. Karl was expected to know how to market and sell and
distribute pianos, take care of the financial picture, invest wisely in

new plants and equipment, and so forth. Only because he demonstrated a possession of the qualities necessary for all of this did the employees of Zoffner Piano come to share in his personal vision and expectations about making excellent instruments at an affordable price. They shared his belief in affordable quality because they believed in the reality of his ability to combine these factors; he had demonstrated it through his words and actions many times. They knew he expected them to make the finest possible pianos, because they knew that, were he able to do so, he would make the finest instruments on his own. They were satisfied with their work when he was satisfied with their work, not necessarily out of a dependence on him for approval but because his standard of excellence set the standard: to be excellent in his eyes was the definition of excellence.

The task of setting direction is thus accomplished, from the perspective of the first principle, by the leader; but the followers' belief in the rightness of that direction depends on qualities that the leader possesses *in the eyes of followers*. This is a key point—even in a leadership principle based on personal dominance, leadership (as opposed to raw coercion) requires a deeply shared understanding.

### Creating Commitment with the First Principle

If we think about commitment as allowing another or others to make a claim on our time, energy, and values, then commitment from the perspective of the first principle is to the leader personally. People commit themselves to the vision, values, beliefs, strategies, and plans of the leader. They allow themselves to be recruited into the leader's world and become citizens of that world. Members of the community or organization commit to one another and to the larger collective through their commitment to the leader. It is in this sense that the leader is often thought of as the glue that holds the organization or community together. Commitment to others in the organization depends on a shared commitment to the leader. Within this principle, it literally makes no sense to be committed to the organization and not be committed to the leader. Commitment to one implies commitment to the other.

Notice how the approach to accomplishing the tasks of setting direction and creating commitment are mutually reinforcing, parts of the same principle. Followers' belief in the direction set by the leader is fundamental to creating commitment. Each follower takes a place within the world, the field of reality and value, created by the leader's vision. All of the places in this world that a follower might take up are defined by the leader's vision of what the community is trying to accomplish. For a follower to fail to commit to an assigned place in this world is not, from the perspective of the first principle, a disagreement with the leader but a refusal of membership in the world created by the leader.

As creator and continuing source of validation for a world that followers inhabit, the leader, from the perspective of the first principle, is accorded extraordinary loyalty. It was so for Mr. Karl. The workers of Zoffner Piano felt they owed him something. But what? Had they not been fairly compensated for their labor all those years? Had they not through their work enriched Mr. Karl and the Zoffner family? Cannot a case be made that Mr. Karl had in fact been exploiting them all this time? To see this relationship as exploitative and to fail to appreciate the sense of loyalty the employees felt for Mr. Karl is to miss the reciprocity of relations involved in the first principle. Commitment and loyalty, like belief in the vision and direction, is a two-way street here. Just as the employees of Zoffner Piano commit to Mr. Karl, so he commits to them, allowing them to make a claim on him—that he live up to their belief in him, that he continually create and re-create the world they inhabit. This is just what he has taken away in retiring and what Elena cannot replace.

Of course, exploitation does happen. Unscrupulous people do take advantage of others. Such exploitation, however, can be distinguished from a context in which the leader and the followers reciprocally share a common knowledge principle (in this case of leadership) that allows them to create and share a world that makes sense to all of them. Much of ineffective leadership can perhaps be accounted for by the attempts of a person to *be* a leader (for example, a dominant leader) without, as it were, *becoming* such a leader—in effect expecting the followers to play their part without fulfilling the leader's part of the relationship, without reciprocity, without actually making common sense.

### Facing Adaptive Challenges with the First Principle

Think back to the distinction between routine challenges and adaptive challenges described in Chapter One—between those challenges a community or organization already understands and for which it is prepared in some way and those challenges that overwhelm the community or organization. Adaptive challenges are the ones that cause confusion about the nature and extent of any problem, creating uncertainty about how to respond and requiring a basic change, an adaptation, in the community or organization.

From the perspective afforded by the personal dominance principle, a community or organization faces adaptive challenges when the leader faces those challenges. The collective capacity to face adaptive challenges depends on the leader's capacity to face such challenges. Thus when some problem or event emerges that is confusing, for which the community has no existing resources for responding, it is the leader who absorbs the shock, sorts through the confusion, decides just what kind of challenge this is, what possible responses exist, and reorients the community with respect to the new demands being placed on it. The community or organization is buffered from the adaptive challenge by the leader, and as a result followers are not usually aware that they have faced an adaptive challenge—they have not experienced the confusion and ambiguity that the leader may have gone through.

At Zoffner Piano, Mr. Karl's first encounter with a digital keyboard a number of years back caused him quite a shock. Here was a product that could quite literally change the face of his market. Inexpensive and loaded with extra features not found on a piano, it seemed to be aimed right at the sons and daughters of those ordinary workers Zoffner Piano hoped would be strong customers. But would people see them as an alternative to a piano or simply as another musical instrument to own in addition to a piano? What was the challenge? How should he respond? Finally he decided that the digital keyboard would be seen as a toy by most people, whereas a piano is a real instrument. This is the story he told his employees. Digital keyboards were understood as toys and therefore could not compete with the pianos they were making. Carry on as always, was his comforting message to them.

Again we see the reciprocity between the dominant leader and followers. The leader absorbs the shock and confusion of an adaptive challenge and supplies a way to respond that is within the capacity of the community or organization, including the leader. Followers retell this story to one another and legitimize it; it takes its place among their beliefs and values and shapes their actions. At Zoffner, Mr. Karl emphasized that if they were to continue to differentiate their product from this digital toy, it was critical to find ways to increase the quality of their product while holding down costs. The company responded by increasing its productivity to record levels. In the years following the introduction of digital keyboards, Zoffner Piano recorded all-time highs in sales and profits. The company had successfully responded to the adaptive challenge. Or at least it had postponed the challenge.

In effect, the leader adapts personally to the challenge and then teaches the community or organization how to adapt. A key point here is that the leader does not adapt personally in just any possible way. The leader must adapt in ways that followers will be able to learn, in ways that followers can follow.

Except for the introduction of digital keyboards, the history of Zoffner Piano up until now has been one of predictable challenges: competitors have entered the scene, recessions have cut into revenues, changes in the cost of materials have tightened margins, trade-offs in the company's quality-to-price formula have changed. All these challenges have fallen well within the capacity of Mr. Karl and the organization to respond to without making fundamental changes. Even the adaptive challenge posed by digital keyboards was faced successfully, at least for a time. This cannot be said of Mr. Karl's retirement, Elena's succession, and her decision to move Zoffner itself into digital technology. How can the story that digital instruments are toys keep making sense now that Zoffner will make them? The company is facing an adaptive challenge like none before, and no one, not even Elena herself, believes that Elena can adapt this one on behalf of the company. Let's return to Zoffner and see what is happening as this crisis of leadership unfolds.

*Even though Elena told her father that she couldn't be like him, she knew that in some ways she would have to emulate him if she was going to solve the problems that were emerging at Zoffner Piano. With employee morale dipping low for the first time in the company's history, people didn't know which way to turn. A few people had taken early retirement and a few had quit. Fortunately most had stayed on for now, but they were increasingly worried and confused. Conversation at lunch and in the shops was filled with speculation and rumor. Their distress began to show up quickly in quality measures—increased rework, scrap, customer complaints. Elena knew that it would take only a few months of this to hurt the Zoffner name, perhaps forever. She responded forcefully.*

*What was needed, she decided, was a new vision for Zoffner. This new vision should be based on her father's original vision, but should bring it up to date in some significant ways to include her plan to move into digital technology. After a week or so of playing around with various ideas, words, and phrases, she came up with this: Zoffner stands for affordable quality keyboard instruments.*

*She had a local advertising agency draw up some "comps" of this with appropriate graphic design and presented it to the management group at their next meeting. What followed was the hardest two hours Elena had ever been through. After her presentation was greeted with nothing more than polite—if uncomfortable—silence, she insisted that people say what they really thought about her vision for the company. It was a difficult conversation to get started, but once people got warmed up, Elena's vision provoked a flood of thoughts and feelings. Here is a summary of the reactions and questions and Elena's responses.*

*"Keyboard instruments doesn't sound like a piano, it sounds like a kid's toy."*

*Elena: We are diversifying, moving away from our sole reliance on the piano. We need to reflect this in our vision.*

*"What does affordable quality mean?"*

*Elena: It means we will make instruments to the customer's standards of quality—neither more quality than they want and need and can afford, nor less.*

*"Then what happens to our own standards? What happens to our pride of craftsmanship?"*

*Elena: We need to realize that the customer pays the bill and it is the customer who ultimately decides what is high quality with respect to a certain price. I expect us to continue to be proud of our work in every way. Serving the needs of the customer shouldn't affect our sense of craftsmanship.*

*"Will we make toy keyboards?"*

*Elena: That depends on your definition of a toy. We will probably manufacture keyboards for kids, yes. Instruments to introduce young people to music and to the Zoffner brand. I want to make it clear that the craftspeople involved in the manufacture of our pianos will continue to do just that. We will be opening a new plant and hiring new workers for the digital line.*

*"How will your new approach to affordable quality affect our pianos?"*

*Elena: Market surveys tell us that our pianos are getting out of the range of the very people my father was aiming at in the first place. The average working person cannot afford to buy one of our pianos as he envisioned. We will be launching a major R&D initiative to develop a Zoffner piano that is just as good as ever at a lower price.*

*"Just as good as what?"*

*Elena: Just as good in the eyes of the customer.*

*And finally, this question: "I notice your vision refers to Zoffner, not Zoffner Piano. Are we changing our name?"*

*Elena: I have filed papers to rename the company Zoffner Music, Inc. This reflects the fact that we will no longer simply be in the piano business. We're in the business of music. This is something we should all feel very excited and energized about. It is a new day and great things lie ahead for us. I expect everyone in this room to communicate that message throughout the organization and to help everyone understand our new vision and their part in it.*

The aftermath of this watershed meeting was no less than catastrophic. Within an hour, three of the top craftspeople in the piano shops resigned, along with the vice president of sales and marketing. These resignations created a sense of panic in the company that Elena was just barely able to quell. She heard reports that many people were looking for new jobs, mostly those who had worked for Zoffner for twenty years or more. Maybe this was as it should be, she told herself. Maybe we need to move forward with younger people who have a better sense of today's realities. But she was worried. She knew that she might have set off the downfall of her father's company.

## The Limits of Personal Dominance

The first leadership principle is a way of understanding leadership, complete in itself. Its basic logic presupposes—and relies on—the presence of a dominant leader and the presence of followers who believe in the leader; without such a leader and without such followers, leadership is not possible. This logic is the very essence of the first principle and also defines its limits. Because the first principle organizes taken-for-granted truths about the personal origin and nature of leadership, its key limits also tend to be personal in nature, starting with the kind of situation we are seeing at Zoffner.

When, for whatever reason, the person of the leader is taken away from the community or organization, leadership as understood from the perspective of the first principle is threatened. There is a leadership vacuum that is also a legitimacy vacuum and a power vacuum. The crisis is created not by the style or character of the lost leader and not by the nature or abilities of those left behind, but by the principle of leadership being used by the group to understand leadership. It is a crisis born of the group's epistemology, its way of knowing. So long as group members continue to understand leadership from the perspective afforded by the first principle, the presence of a dominant leader will be required, and they will experience the loss of the leader as a loss of leadership for which the only possible remedy is to find yet another dominant leader. This is sometimes possible, and leadership is regained. Often, however, the interrelationship of a particular leader and a particular community of followers has created a context that no new leader can step into—the relationship between dominant leader and followers is unique to that particular leader, those particular followers. A new leader fails simply because no newcomer can re-create that unique relationship. Then the community or organization is in extreme danger of losing its way for lack of leadership.

The question of whether leadership is a general ability (one that a person can take from one community or organization to another) finds at least a hint of an answer in thinking about this limit of personal dominance. First, the question itself may take a first-principle view of leadership, seemingly assuming as it does that leadership is a personal ability. Granting this as true, one could answer that whether such an ability can be generalized depends on the extent to which, in a new community, the reciprocal sense-making patterns required for the first principle to make leadership happen can be created. As we have seen, this is not something that the leader does alone: the patterns are reciprocal and require the participation of followers as well as the leader. So whether leadership ability is a general (and personal) trait would seem to depend on the nature of an interrelationship in which the leader plays only one (albeit a critical) part.

Because personal dominance depends on this interrelationship between dominant leader and followers who believe in that dominance, the loss of key followers also threatens the capacity of the first principle to make leadership happen. Belief in the rightness of the leader's direction, commitment through loyalty to the leader, the willingness to face challenges as the leader faces them are all, as we have seen, indispensable aspects of personal dominance. Without followers who take up these aspects of the interrelationship, leadership fails to materialize. And when followers who have in the past played their part in this reciprocity, for whatever reasons, withdraw their belief, their loyalty, their dependence on the leader, the personal dominance principle reaches its limit as surely as when the leader is lost.

Followers may withdraw from the interrelationship for a variety of reasons. The leader might act so as to violate the followers' sense of personal loyalty, undermining the basis of commitment. Or a leader might set a very bad direction or fail to recognize and face a key challenge, causing followers to lose their belief in the leader's dominance.

These are merely incidental happenstance that may be avoided. The psychological development of followers, on the other hand, may create a more inexorable movement toward the limits of the first principle. As followers mature personally and develop a sense of having a unique self-authored identity, they may begin to question their reliance on the leader for the accomplishment of the leadership tasks. Followers can begin to demand that they be included somehow in accomplishing the leadership tasks. This can be seen as a threat by the leader and might be dealt with as such, maintaining at least for a while the sensemaking capacity of personal dominance. It is when this psychological movement on the part of followers results not in pushing back against the leader but in choosing to stop following that the first principle again begins to reach its limits.

Finally, the leader may come in time through personal psychological development to recognize that the leadership tasks are beyond the power of a single person to accomplish. The leader may come to view the individual accomplishment of the leadership tasks as a kind of unwarranted and excessive pride, or may more practically come to see that the inclusion of followers in decisions is likely to create better decisions.

Some complex combination of these kinds of limits seems apparent at Zoffner. Mr. Karl has retired, the leader has been lost. But Elena has shown herself willing to at least try to take his place as the dominant leader; she is trying to take up the part of the leader from the perspective that has for so long afforded the company its understanding of leadership. Yet her efforts are not being met with a reciprocal response—the managers are not taking up the part of followers, so the followers have in this sense also been lost. Thus Elena's attempt to become personally dominant is failing not because of her lack of leadership ability but more widely because of a breakdown in the ability of the first principle to make sense. This breakdown is captured in the commonsense adage that for a leader to lead, followers must follow.

The outcome of reaching these kinds of limits is that the leadership tasks cannot be accomplished effectively. Let's look at each of the leadership tasks again and see how the first principle can lose its power to accomplish the tasks and thus reach the limits of its usefulness.

## Limits in Setting Direction

We have seen how the personally dominant leader is understood to know what is right, so that the direction the leader supplies is one that followers can and do believe in. Whenever this understanding is threatened, the first principle is in danger of reaching the limit of its power to make leadership happen. What kinds of contexts might arise that would threaten this way of understanding leadership?

The most obvious involves a significant increase in complexity. When the context in which a community or organization operates becomes so complex that the leader cannot personally discern all the factors that could potentially go into choosing a direction that followers can believe in, an effective direction can become elusive. What happens then? What happens when the dominant leader chooses a direction that followers do not and cannot believe in? The community and the leader are faced with a situation for which their shared understanding of leadership has only a few answers. One of the answers afforded from the perspective of the first principle is that the leader is not a true leader, not really equipped for the demands of the role: not smart enough or powerful enough or resourceful enough. Another way that the principle could make sense of this situation, and one that maintains the legitimacy of the leader (and is therefore probably used more often), is to say that the leader is a true leader but the followers have failed the leader in some way. Their failure to believe in the leader's direction indicates that they do not fully understand the direction, or it indicates a lack of imagination, or that they are resistant to change. Either way, the dominance principle makes sense most readily of such a failure by identifying a cause for the failure either in the leader or in the followers.

The logic of the dominance principle fails to make sense of (fails to see as leadership) a direction that is ambiguous with respect to its power to inspire the belief of followers. A direction that is unclear is a paradox from the perspective of the first principle. This sense of paradox is directly attributable to the limits of the principle. The dominance principle fails to make leadership happen when there is no clear choice of direction, so that no direction will seem to be definitely "right," or where all choices are to some degree flawed. In such a situation, no matter what direction the leader sets, some blame will have to be attached either to the leader or the followers. These situations are *fundamentally* problematic from the perspective afforded by the personal dominance principle. In the face of these built-in limitations, the capacity of the community or organization to stay together is threatened; constant internal conflicts hang over everyone's head—the center (the dominant leader) cannot hold.

Such is the context in which Zoffner Music is now trying to operate. The new direction articulated by Elena is not at all clear. What does it mean to change from making high-quality instruments that are affordable to making instruments of affordable quality? What does it mean to change from being in the business of making pianos to being in the music business? What does it mean to put the Zoffner name on digital keyboards? No one can answer these questions. Most important for the future efficacy of the personal dominance principle as a way of understanding leadership at Zoffner, Elena cannot answer them. They are questions whose answers must be discovered as the company moves in their direction. This is a fundamentally different way of thinking about direction than that afforded by the first principle. The leadership crisis at Zoffner is a crisis of ways of knowing; the limits of the first principle have been reached and exceeded; some new way of understanding leadership is being called forth.

## Limits in Creating Commitment

From the perspective afforded by the first principle, people commit directly to the leader; commitment to others in the community or organization and commitment to the community or organization as an abstraction (feeling committed to "us") depends on people being committed to, loyal to, the leader. This commitment and loyalty is reciprocal. Just as followers allow the leader to make a claim on them, the leader allows followers to make their own claim on the leader for guidance, protection, and identity. What is the built-in limitation of this? What contexts might arise that would significantly limit the power of the first principle to accomplish the leadership task of creating commitment?

One such context is evident in the Zoffner story—when a person takes on the role of dominant leader but followers are unwilling to enter into a reciprocally committed relationship with the new leader, leadership does not happen. More about that a little later. Another context that does not involve a change in the leader can come about when the leader fails in some way that violates the followers' investment of loyalty. For example, if the dominant leader should take advantage of that loyalty—that is, misuse the trust of followers, show duplicity of some kind, or otherwise fail to uphold the leader's part of the reciprocal relationship. When the leader's part in the relationship is withdrawn, the whole system comes down and commitment is threatened; the capacity of people to allow the leader to make a claim on them is reduced or eliminated altogether.

The perspective afforded by the first principle does not make sense of followers' committing to one another or to the organization as an abstraction without the presence of the leader to act as a focal point for that commitment. When the leader somehow violates the commitment and loyalty of followers, the first principle becomes powerless to accomplish the leadership task of creating commitment. People who understand leadership from the perspective of the first principle experience this as a loss of the leader and thus a loss of leadership. The principle provides no alternative way to understand how commitment could be created.

We can see the difficulty Elena faces. How can she create commitment (how can commitment be created in the company) given the fact that the employees are *unwilling* to allow her to make a claim on them and, because she cannot effectively set direction, she is *unable* to allow them to make a claim on her for guidance and direction? As we saw before, the situation seems hopeless from the perspective afforded by the first principle. Once again, we can sense that some different leadership principle is being called forth.

### Limits in Facing Adaptive Challenges

The third leadership task involves facing, responding to, dealing with adaptive challenges. By definition, an adaptive challenge involves the need to understand and interpret events that lie outside a person's existing frameworks for making sense of what is happening. This includes even the most intelligent and resourceful of leaders. If the challenge is adaptive, the leader will be significantly confused, lack understanding, have no way of interpreting what kind of challenge this is, will not know how to respond, and will not know how to teach the community or organization how to respond. This would seem to be the most difficult leadership task to accomplish from the perspective afforded by the first principle.

To accomplish this task, leadership from the perspective of the first principle depends on the legitimacy of the leader in the eyes of followers. The dominant leader is accorded the legitimacy of defining what is real, what is happening, what it means. From the perspective afforded by the first principle, then, the dominant leader can face an adaptive challenge—one for which the leader is no more prepared than any of the followers—as Mr. Karl did, by assimilating the challenge to existing tools for responding. Zoffner was prepared for competition from "real" pianos, so by defining digital keyboards as "toys" Mr. Karl eliminated them as a source of competition. This way of accomplishing this leadership task is limited by the usefulness of such a redefinition of an adaptive challenge. In the case of Zoffner, it worked at least up until the retirement of Mr. Karl. Somehow, however, the digital keyboard did not go away and now it is coming back to confront not just Elena but, it would seem, all of them. The context has shifted significantly. The employees are no longer buffered from this adaptive challenge. They are facing it themselves. They are themselves confused, threatened, their sense of identity undermined. It would seem that the leadership task of facing adaptive challenges cannot be accomplished without some different way of understanding leadership itself.

What happens in an organization making sense of leadership from the perspective of the first principle when that principle begins to routinely encounter its limits of sensemaking? We have seen that leadership is lost; the community or organization cannot see that leadership is happening. How do people respond to this loss? They more than likely respond from within the perspective of the principle itself. The sensemaking of the principle with respect to its own limits creates some of the following interpretations of those limits:

- Followers are not understanding the leader, and the leader needs to communicate better, more often, more clearly.

- Followers are doubting the leader, and the leader needs to demonstrate a continuing capacity to keep up with the job.

- Followers are challenging the authority of the leader, and the leader needs to reassert dominance.

If the leader does not come up with actions that make sense within these interpretations, the obvious corollary is that a new leader is needed.

This means that situations in which followers fail to understand the leader, or in which followers disagree with the leader, or in which followers challenge the actions of the leader are *fundamentally* problematic situations from the perspective of the first principle. They are situations in which the very capacity of the principle to bring leadership into being is reaching significant limitations. Doubting or challenging the leader strikes at the very heart of the principle itself.

## Why Is It Important to Understand the Limits of a Principle?

Why has so much time been spent discussing the limits of the personal dominance principle? Is it because it is a flawed principle or because it is an outmoded way of thinking about leadership or because it is likely to lead to the empowerment of those already in power? No. The personal dominance principle is often an effective way to understand leadership and thus bring leadership into being. But in many contexts arising in today's complex communities and organizations, the limits of the first principle are encountered more and more frequently. People in such communities and organizations need some way of thinking about leadership that overcomes the limitations of the personal dominance principle. Before discussing how this can happen, let's review the capacities (what the principle affords people in making sense of leadership) and the limits (how the principle fails to make sense of leadership) of personal dominance as related to the leadership tasks.

Limits are a normal and inescapable aspect of any knowledge principle. Any way of understanding leadership will afford ways of making sense in certain contexts that will fail to make sense of other contexts. The limits of the dominance principle, as summarized in Table 2.1, are likely to be encountered from time to time in communities organizing their thinking about leadership in this way. Occasional limit-testing events are not a long-term threat to the usefulness of the principle. A dominant leader who lacks sufficient knowledge on occasion still has ways of regaining legitimacy. Failures to deserve the loyalty, even the respect, of followers can be

**Table 2.1  Capacities and Limits of the Personal Dominance Principle with Respect to the Leadership Tasks**

| Tasks | Capacities of Personal Dominance | Limits of Personal Dominance |
|---|---|---|
| Setting direction | The leader is understood to possess as a personal quality the knowledge of what is needed and the right thing to do. | Increasing complexity or changes in context impede the leader from knowing the right direction, and followers lose their belief in the leader's ability to lead. |
| Creating commitment | Followers commit to the leader personally (they are loyal to the leader) and commit to one another by virtue of their commitment to the leader. | When the leader fails personally to deserve the commitment and loyalty of followers, commitment to the community or organization overall is threatened. |
| Facing adaptive challenge | The leader adapts personally and teaches the community or organization how to adapt; followers adapt as the leader adapts. | When challenges arise that the leader cannot adapt to personally, the community or organization fails to adapt. |

reversed by a dominant leader if they happen only rarely; so long as there are not too many challenges that lie outside the capacity of the leader to recognize and adapt to them, the capacity for the community to adapt is not permanently impaired.

But what if the context of the community or organization changes in ways that make these limit-testing events more than occasional interruptions? What happens when the limits of a principle such as the personal dominance principle begin to be approached more often than not? Because the very purpose of the principle is to make sense of things—to make things understandable and meaningful to people—when it begins as a matter of course to fail to do this, people begin to search for some other way to gain a sense of understanding and meaning. Under what circumstances might the limits of the personal dominance principle tend to be routinely encountered so that people understanding leadership according to its logic would begin to search for a new and more meaningful principle?

There are two ways to think about this question. One is to take a historical perspective, and the other involves a personal perspective.

### Historical Perspective on the Limits of the First Principle

From the historical perspective, the personal dominance principle can be understood as the foundational principle for rule by pharaohs, kings, princes, priests, and other examples of a ruling class. In its most striking form, for example, this principle applies to the way of understanding a pharaoh as a god. A leader who is understood to be a god possesses the characteristics of personal dominance in absolute form: what such a leader says is not only true, it literally defines what is real and unambiguously articulates what is important, what is right, what is just.

Imagine for a moment living in the condition in which you deeply believed that the leader of your community was a god or was godlike. Whenever a difficult moral or ethical question arose in the community, one that perhaps was dividing people, causing conflict and confusion, a powerful resource could be brought to bear in the form of the leader's unquestioned (because unquestionable) capacity to say what was the case, to resolve the moral question. This kind of moral certainty reminds one of the story of Solomon and the dispute over the baby. The power of this story resides at least in part in our fascination over the power of Solomon to threaten to cleave the infant on the spot, thus revealing the true mother. Imagine this same dispute playing out in our modern courts, where the legal wrangling might go on for years while the baby and the real mother (and the putative mother) continued to suffer. But Solomon possessed a power unknown today, and the source of the power was rooted in the whole constructed logic of the personal dominance principle: as king he had not just the right to say what was just, he had a position wherein it made sense for him and him alone to say what was just. Any other means of determining justice would have failed the test of meaningfulness.

From our point of view (being thoroughly embedded in a society where rule by godlike humans has become impossible for nearly everyone) such an idea of leadership seems to require that the followers of the day were the victims of brutal repression to be so utterly subject to the words and whims of a ruler. And yet if the only principle for understanding leadership that was widely available was the personal dominance principle, then people who would make sense of pharaohs and kings had very little choice—to understand their lives, they employed the logic available. From that logic, pharaohs and kings and other rulers ruled by virtue of some personal ascendancy over others, who were understood to be more ordinary, more simply human. This logic was supported by most of the institutions and beliefs of the times. In the thirteenth century, for example, the churchman and philosopher Roger Bacon proposed the creation of a worldwide society of Christians under the leadership of the Pope. The idea of the whole world's being led by a single person was at least thinkable.

In time, of course, the logic of personal dominance began to lose its power to make sense of kings and of the idea of universal leadership. Surely by the time of the Enlightenment and the age of rationalism the limits of the personal dominance principle were being reached on a routine basis in many contexts of social activity. As the idea arose that the ordinary person could by the power of the individual mind go out into the world and observe nature and draw conclusions from those observations and from those conclusions create knowledge, the idea that some people were inherently ascendant began to make less and less sense. If the ordinary person could understand the glory of nature and create knowledge, what use was there in having someone who claimed to have special access to knowledge? If values and beliefs could be thought through by the ordinary person based on personal experience, what sense did it make to take the word of a king on matters of morals and ethics? If the ordinary person could marshal facts and feelings in support of a decision, what meaning was there in turning over the power of deciding to someone who might not have one's best interests at heart?

## Personal Perspective on the Limits of the First Principle

With these kinds of questions in mind, let's turn from the historical perspective to the personal one. As suggested earlier, the personal dominance principle can be understood as the foundational principle by which we humans begin our understanding of leadership: as a young child a person sees parents as dominant figures, then teachers, mentors, the first boss, and so forth. But the first principle is not a childish way of understanding leadership. As an adult, a person can live and work in contexts that support the meaningfulness of the first principle, its capacity to accomplish the leadership tasks. This was true of many if not most of the individual employees of Zoffner Piano. It was probably not because of Mr. Karl's fatherly appearance alone that people thought of him as a father figure. For many of them he took the part of a father in the sense that he contributed to their sense of self. Like a father, he was for many people a source of values, of right and wrong, of what it meant to be a craftsman. The context supported people in defining themselves in relation to such a figure.

But a person who continues to mature may in time create an identity independent of a dominant figure, even a benevolent and effective dominant figure such as Mr. Karl. With the development of experience and understanding in terms not set by such a figure, it is natural to begin to lose the sense of that person as being personally dominant. This kind of personal growth among people in a community or organization limits the first principle's capacity to create leadership. Because not everyone in a community or organization will have grown personally to the same degree, with some still effectively understanding leadership from the perspective of the first principle and others losing that meaning of leadership, people in a complex organization are likely to organize the very idea of leadership in basically different ways. They do not merely have differing definitions of leadership, they know and recognize leadership differently. This idea that communities and organizations comprise a variety of ways of knowing leadership will become more important as we move into a discussion of leadership development in communities and organizations.

Thus in both a historical sense and from a personal point of view, contexts can arise in which the sensemaking of the first principle is inadequate to the demands of the leadership tasks.

### How Can the Limits of the First Principle Be Addressed?

To approach the question of addressing the first principle's limits, let's try to answer the one I asked at the beginning of this chapter: What was the essence of Mr. Karl's leadership of Zoffner Piano Company for all those years? The most common way to answer this question is to refer to Mr. Karl's leadership ability. Thus the most common answer to my question is that Mr. Karl possessed a high degree of leadership ability. This answer prompts further questions, such as what is the nature of that ability, how can it be acquired, can we teach other people different from Mr. Karl to have such an ability? These kinds of questions lead us into the field of leadership theory as it has most often been articulated. These questions have proved difficult to answer, and have often caused more confusion about leadership than useful approaches to understanding.

The answer I am suggesting is significantly different. The essence of Mr. Karl's leadership did *not* lie in some ability he possessed. The essence of his leadership lay in the power of a shared knowledge principle to make sense of leadership *in the whole community* of Zoffner Piano Company. It seems, therefore, that we have come to the conclusion that Mr. Karl's highly personal leadership, his personal dominance, was rooted in a shared knowledge principle. Personal leadership, from this viewpoint, is *shared leadership,* because for it to be effective, everyone had to make sense of leadership from the perspective afforded by the same principle. Had there been a significant number of people who did not make sense of leadership from this perspective (as is more usually the case), then Mr. Karl's leadership would not have had the same power to make sense in the community overall. "His" leadership would have been far less effective. This brings us to a key hypothesis of this book. *All leadership is shared leadership*. Even the most highly dominant forms of leadership—that of the godlike pharaohs included— can be usefully understood as forms of shared leadership.

Where does this leave Elena in her struggle to provide leadership for Zoffner Piano? In her belief that to be an effective leader she must emulate her father, she is trying to articulate a new direction, create new commitments, and face an adaptive challenge from the perspective provided by the personal dominance principle. And yet, we must ask, To what extent does that principle make sense of leadership in the context emerging after Mr. Karl's retirement? When there is significant ambiguity and complexity, setting a direction that is understood to be "right" borders on the impossible; people cannot believe in the direction and hence cannot believe in the capacity of the leader to set direction. The old loyalty and commitment to Mr. Karl cannot easily be transferred to Elena; people are left with very little basis for maintaining their commitment to the company without Mr. Karl in charge. Instead of facing an adaptive challenge on behalf of the company, Elena is asking its people to adapt themselves to new challenges along with her—she cannot adapt unless they also adapt. If the hypothesis of this book is a useful way to look at this situation, we see that what is needed at Zoffner is not leadership development for Elena, it is the development of the whole leadership principle by which the company makes leadership make sense, by which it understands that the leadership tasks are getting accomplished. To make leadership work again at Zoffner, leadership development will have to involve everyone.

## Chapter Three

# Interpersonal Influence

*Elena began to change her mind about leadership after a long conversation she had with Raul, the new director of marketing she hired to replace the long-time director who resigned. Raul had an MBA from an Ivy League school and fifteen years' experience in marketing in two large corporations. He was worldly wise, as Elena saw it, and it wasn't long before she was seeking out his advice about her struggles in taking over from her father. Raul brought a new set of eyes to the situation, and he had a way of asking questions that were a little uncomfortable but helpful.*

*"Why are you trying to be like your father?"*

*"I'm not. I could never be like him. What I am trying to do is provide leadership to this company. But I'm afraid I simply can't do it. I don't have what it takes."*

*"Why do you say that?"*

*"People here just don't see me as a leader. I'm still my father's little girl to them and I'll never be anything else. It's frustrating because I feel responsible for the leadership, but I can't fulfill my responsibility."*

*"Maybe if you took a different approach. Like trying to get the managers involved more. Let them participate more. Sure, your father ruled like a king, but I think it's more effective for you to try being open to their participation."*

*"But that's just it. They don't want to participate."*

*"What about changing the management committee to something like the leadership council? Let them know you want them to be a part of the leadership of the company, not just managers who carry out your plans. Open things up to more discussion of ideas. Brainstorming pros and cons, considering alternatives, that kind of thing. We need more people in this company acting like leaders. You can't do it alone."*

*Elena was doubtful about this approach. She knew these people, and they were primarily interested in doing a good job, drawing a good paycheck, and going home. They were managers now, but for most of their working lives they had been on the shop floor—craftsmen, builders, doers. They weren't that interested in thinking about the business in strategic terms. They would see that as an added burden on them. Even so, she was frustrated enough with their attitude about her that she was willing to try anything, even if its only purpose was to shake things up. So she did what Raul suggested. One day at a management committee meeting she announced that the group would henceforth be known as the leadership council. She said it was because she wanted them to be more than just managers from now on.*

*"I want each of you to be a leader in this company." In spite of her own doubts and the looks on their faces, she sensed there was something right about these words. It felt good to say this to them. Put some of the responsibility for leadership on them instead of trying to be the only leader.*

*Looking back years later, she could laugh at how little effect it had on the people in the room at the time. They took it as yet another of her pronouncements and gave it little thought. In truth, she didn't pay it much more attention than they did. At least not at first. But it was how they all began to change their minds about leadership.*

## The Meaning of the Second Principle

When Mr. Karl retired, a knowledge principle retired with him. It is not gone yet, of course, because people in the company are still holding a view of leadership based on the first principle. But from that view of leadership, leadership has vanished. And because sooner or later the leadership tasks of setting direction, creating commitment, and facing adaptive challenges must be accomplished if Zoffner is to survive and begin to flourish again, one of two things must happen. Either Mr. Karl must be successfully replaced, or the personal dominance principle itself must be replaced.

What would it mean to replace Mr. Karl? From one point of view—the idea that leadership is the quality of a dominant person—a replacement for Mr. Karl might be found. Someone with knowledge of piano making and with the leadership ability required to lead a company like Zoffner could, according to this view, come in and take charge and accomplish the leadership tasks. If Mr. Karl had not made it clear that Elena was to take over for him, this probably would have been tried. But from the point of view being presented in this book, Mr. Karl cannot be replaced. Because leadership is viewed as arising in a shared knowledge principle, leadership was not *in* Mr. Karl. Leadership was in the *sharing of a way of knowing leadership* between Mr. Karl and the employees of the company. This shared creation of leadership was worked out through years of experience with one another and cannot simply be reproduced by replacing Mr. Karl with some other presumed leader. Lacking the shared history of experience and relationship, a new leader would face the same kinds of obstacles to re-creating personal dominance that Elena faces. Only Mr. Karl could ever play the perfectly attuned reciprocal part in the shared production of leadership at Zoffner. And only those employees could play their part in perfect step with Mr. Karl. It is precisely in this sense that Mr. Karl becomes personally dominant. I believe this is what creates the sense of charisma that often goes along with personal dominance. Dominance and charisma come from this perfect attunement between leader and follower in the shared creation of a kind of leadership that creates a leader who is irreplaceable. (The fact that the followers are also irreplaceable is of course usually overlooked in discussions of leadership.)

If Mr. Karl is irreplaceable, if the followers that created leadership in attunement with Mr. Karl are left without a meaningful partner, then it would seem to spell the end of the personal dominance principle in the company. So long as leadership is sought from the perspective afforded by the first principle, leadership will not be found. Leadership is not missing because Elena is failing to provide it, as she and others think, but because it cannot be seen from the viewpoint people are taking. To find leadership again, some new viewpoint must be taken. The perspective afforded by some different leadership principle is required. But it is not enough that this new principle be different; it must address the particular limitations of the personal dominance principle that are causing leadership to disappear.

In summary, all leadership, including the most highly personal kind, is shared leadership because leadership is a feature of a social system. Even leadership like that provided by Mr. Karl is the product of a shared knowledge principle and thus can be usefully understood as a shared achievement of Zoffner Piano Company, not just an expression of Mr. Karl's personal magnetism.

From this perspective, Elena's change in approach to leadership, then, is not explained as a change in her leadership style—the more expected interpretation of what is happening. Instead, her change in approach to leadership is understood as the development of a qualitatively more complex leadership principle within Zoffner. The introduction of the idea of a leadership council and Elena's proposal that the managers should begin to act like leaders will strike a false note at first and for so long as she and they continue to make sense of leadership from the perspective of personal dominance. The idea of a leadership council and more people acting like leaders is at this point something of a Trojan horse, an idea that is perceived as nothing more than rhetoric but one that as time goes by will begin to come to life, will begin to be understood as a replacement for personal dominance as a way to make sense of leadership.

The second leadership principle, then, is not just any principle. It replaces the first principle in particular ways. Specifically, it holds onto aspects of the first principle that are still useful in making leadership happen again—in accomplishing the leadership tasks—and goes beyond, transcends, the aspects of the first principle that have shown significant limitations in making leadership happen. In this way the second principle is a *development on* the first principle. Because it is a development on the first principle—in some ways containing the first principle while overcoming its limitations—it is more complex than the first principle. As we will see, being more complex has both advantages and disadvantages.

The second principle organizes new truths about leadership, truths that take into account the experience of reaching the limits of the first principle and that search for more encompassing ways of recognizing leadership, richer ways of understanding how the leadership tasks can be accomplished. The second principle begins in the attempt to overcome the limits of the first and goes on to build its own unique meaning for leadership, its own set of taken-for-granted truths. How might the taken-for-granted truths of the second principle be articulated?

## Leadership Is a Process of Social Influence

In some sense, the new truths of the second principle begin with Copernicus. When the earth stopped being understood as the center of the universe and the movement of the stars became a matter of the movement of the observer, a profoundly new idea was introduced. This new idea was that the apparent nature of the objective world is determined by the nature and condition of the observer. In other words, reality is not simply *there*. It must be observed and there must be an observer, and the nature and perspective of the observer makes a difference in what is observed.

Each person's mind is a receptor, or a mirror, in which what is real is caught or reflected. The claims of all kinds of authorities to ultimate knowledge are brought into question by this idea. If each person has some unique view of the world, then each person potentially has a piece of the truth about the world. And no one would seem to have the whole truth. To get at the whole truth, people need to see things from more than one perspective and try to integrate what is best in those perspectives.

Truth is thus no longer the sole possession of certain specially endowed people. *What to do, where to go, how to get there* are all seen as things that no one person can necessarily know. Instead it becomes something that is open to question, open to some process of reasoning and argument among many people. It is not the quality of dominance that counts so much in leadership—the ability to put ideas into the heads of followers—but the quality of being able to persuade others. Leadership in this view involves the ability to *shape and use* ideas that people already have and hold dear, the ability to connect the various truths that individuals hold dear into a larger truth that people can believe in as a community and that they can hold in common.

The process by which people attempt to elevate their own vision of what is real (what is important, what is valuable) to a higher, more collective understanding is a process of creating meaning by negotiating influence. Where personal dominance emphasizes the inner quality of the leader, interpersonal influence emphasizes the relationship among the hearts and minds of people in a community. Where dominant leadership is a quality of a special person, leadership now becomes a social process of negotiating influence.

### The Leader Is the One with the Most Influence

Then in what sense does a leader keep the distinction between leader and follower? If leaders and followers interact and mutually influence one another, in what way does the perspective of the second principle afford an understanding that the leader is different from followers, that the leader can usefully be identified as a leader?

From the perspective of the second principle, the difference between a leader and a follower is in the relative degree of mutual influence: the leader influences followers more than followers influence the leader. Identifying the person with the most influence over others identifies the leader.

Thus, from the perspective afforded by the second principle, a leader can emerge as conditions change because changing conditions can alter the flow of influence and reconstitute someone formerly a follower as the current leader. This can happen, for example, when a crisis arises and someone emerges as the leader by virtue of having more knowledge with respect to the context of the crisis. Also, as the influence flowing between leader and followers approaches equality, it makes less and less sense, from the perspective of the second principle, to understand that leadership is happening. When influence begins to equalize, the logic of the second principle leads people to understand that something like collegiality, mutuality, or consensus is happening and that, at least for that moment, leadership has moved into the background or disappeared altogether.

### The Leader Plays a Role and Acts with Followers

U.S. President Harry Truman once said that leadership was "getting people to do what they don't want to do and like it." Is this an expression of leadership that makes sense from the first principle or from the second? Had he stopped after saying that leadership is getting people to do what they don't want to do, he might have been describing leadership from the perspective of the first principle (or he might have been making an ironic statement—we cannot draw firm conclusions about what principle made sense of leadership for him based on this quote). But he added the words *and like it*. What can we make of this addition? What does it mean to get people to like doing what they don't want to do? It seems to open a door to a whole new world of the psychology of the follower. It seems to say something about the leader getting into the minds of followers, understanding the world from the point of view of followers. The nineteenth-century German philosopher Hegel made just this point when he said that to understand the follower's mind a leader should spend time as a follower. In other words, some kind of empathy for followers is seen as being useful to a leader's effectiveness.

From the perspective afforded by the second principle, leadership is understood to happen when a leader understands and taps into followers' motives for following. Unlike the meaning of the first principle, where the leader acts on followers who respond to the leader personally and directly, the second principle makes sense of leadership when followers respond to the leader not directly but *in relation to their own motives;* the leader must somehow understand motives in followers, win followers over by aligning with their interests and values, and cause them to be persuaded in something like their own terms. Followers in the meantime must also be prepared to play their part by understanding themselves, their values and motives, their reasons for entering into a follower relationship with this leader.

It is in this sense that the leader no longer *acts on* followers but is engaged in acting with followers who are acting with the leader. A dominant leader may think about the motives of followers, but those motives are understood as a factor either favorable or resistant to the leader's plans, ideas, goals. The leader *acts on* followers' inner life, taking advantage of it or working around it. The leader is literally charged with the power of action, and followers either move in accord with that power or, as the saying goes, they get out of the way. The idea of *acting with* followers is significantly different. The inner world of motives of followers is not just a fact that may help the leader or get in the way of the leader's plans, it is a reality that affects the leader's plans, ideas, feelings. Followers act with the leader just as the leader acts with them, so that, in seeking to influence followers, the leader opens up to influence from followers. The leader and the followers take on mutually constructive roles.

Because the interpersonal influence principle is familiar to us and seems perhaps somewhat obvious and mundane, it may be hard to imagine the change in understanding that it represents. From a way of understanding leadership as dominance by virtue of the personal qualities possessed by a leader to understanding leadership as influence by virtue of a leader's interpersonal connection is quite a leap, however. I am not saying that a company such as Zoffner Piano takes this leap by going from a context in which leaders don't care about people to one in which leaders do care about people. It is the idea that a mutual interpersonal connection between leader and followers *makes leadership happen* that is the leap. If they are lucky, people always live and work in contexts of interpersonal connection, where they care about one another and use that connection and caring to influence one another. Such interpersonal connection happened at Zoffner Piano under Mr. Karl. He was close friends with any number of his employees and thus knew their hearts and minds. But this knowledge was not an aspect of leadership; this knowledge did nothing to help make leadership happen; if anything, such knowledge made leadership less likely to happen by threatening Mr. Karl's dominance.

The big leap—the development of the leadership principle from the first to the second—involves understanding that *leadership is happening* when interpersonal connection creates mutual influence between a leader and followers. When this happens, people are re-making their sense of leadership; they are letting go of one principle for understanding leadership and taking on a new one. What used to look like leadership (personal dominance) can start to look more like coercion, ineffective leadership, or inappropriate use of power. What looks like leadership now (interpersonal influence) used to be a feature only of relationships among peers or friends, not of those between leaders and followers.

## *The Leadership Role Both Resembles and Differs From Dominance*

Under the second principle, playing the leadership role retains aspects of dominance and also departs in important ways from dominance. Many things count as influence in this way of understanding leadership: knowledge and experience, persuasiveness, intelligence, authority, power, ideas, creativity, and so forth. These are understood as personal qualities of the person, and thus the second principle builds on an important aspect of the first: the leader is a person who has certain kinds of qualities. At the same time, the second principle departs radically from the first in that these qualities do not in themselves constitute leadership—they only enable a person to fill a leadership role. The role itself is an aspect of a relationship in which influence is negotiated. Thus a person becomes a leader as a result of participating in the negotiation of influence.

But what about power? What sense does the second principle make of power in a context of interpersonal influence? The first principle, as we saw, counts on the power of the leader. That power is personal. The sources of power are owned by the leader. Whatever way the leader uses that power is in principle an aspect of leadership. But from the perspective of the second principle, the power of leadership is influence, the ability to connect to, shape, and make use of the perspectives of others. The power of leadership, then, is by definition not that of coercion or force but of connection and relationship. Sources of power, such as those derived from authority and position, increase the influence of a person relative to others and thus contribute to the identification of that person as the leader, but their use, for example, to force compliance with the will of the leader is understood to stand against leadership, to be an abandonment of leadership in favor of mere coercion. The second principle, therefore, interprets power as a tool of the leader (the person playing that role in relation to followers), and one that must be used with sensitivity and care.

### Summary of the Sensemaking
### Change from First to Second Principle

The sensemaking change from the first principle to the second principle transforms the way the leader is understood, the way followers are understood, and the way leadership is recognized as happening. The leader changes from being the person who possesses leadership as a personal quality to being the person who has gained the most influence in a community or organization. The followers change from being people who look to the leader for leadership and are acted on by the leader to being people who understand why they wish to be followers of this leader and who act with the leader. Leadership itself changes from what happens when the leader takes charge to what happens when a leader and followers interact and mutually influence one another, with the leader having more influence than followers.

Before elaborating on this way of understanding leadership, let's stop and ask: Is this second principle what is needed at Zoffner Piano? Is a change in the knowledge principle by which Elena and others in the company recognize leadership required for Elena to become the leader? Can she become the leader even then?

*Every week for more than a year the managers of Zoffner Piano met with Elena under the name of the leadership council. At first this seemed to be the only change, and no one made much of it. Compared with the major changes the company was going through during that time, a mere change of name for the weekly meeting was hardly remarkable.*

*The managers noticed Raul, of course. He spoke up in meetings as often as Elena, and word got around that he was the one really running the company now. The two of them spent a lot of time together and seemed always to be in sync during the leadership council meetings. Elena gave Raul primary responsibility for moving Zoffner into* the digital business. His plan called for the creation of a whole new division with its own plant, employees, distribution channels, and markets.

The new plant would be built on a site adjacent to the existing pianoworks, land that Mr. Karl had purchased years ago for what he always called "the future." The veteran managers understood that by the future he meant a new foundry, new cabinet shops, or an updated freight operation. As the low, sprawling, utterly utilitarian new plant was being built, they shook their heads. They shared an embattled feeling with one another. It was a feeling that slowly began to give them a sense of identity. They began to see themselves as defenders of Zoffner's past, as keepers of an old-world craftsmanship that was being threatened.

Almost casually, one Friday afternoon after work, one of them made a comment that was to have far-ranging consequences in the life of their company.

"I tell you what I think," offered Eddie Stone, who headed up the foundry and who had been with Zoffner for thirty years, "I think this leadership council is probably a sham and maybe Raul is running things, but why do we have to go along with their decisions? We're the ones who have to look out for the real Zoffner. I think we ought to start thinking for ourselves. I think we ought to start standing up for the Zoffner Piano Company we helped build before it goes to hell."

The group sat up at this idea. There were several comments made in agreement. But the idea struck one or two of them as being somehow subversive. "Can we do that?" someone asked. Eddie countered that they couldn't afford not to.

"But it's Elena's company now, Eddie," someone else said. "Mr. Karl turned it over to her and she has a right to run it as she sees fit.

If we don't like what she's doing, we know what we can do. I've been struggling this whole year, thinking about resigning. I don't know what I'd do if I left, and that's why I've stayed so far; but I won't be party to any kind of behind-the-back stuff."

"I'm not talking about going around Elena and Raul," Eddie explained, "I'm talking about being heard. It's time for us to speak up for our values and not just sit there and let Elena and Raul make decisions that affect all of us without offering any resistance."

Nan, the financial officer, agreed. "Why would we need to go behind anyone's back? We sit in there week after week with our mouths shut. All we have to do is open up and talk."

"And say what, exactly? I mean, just what is our place there? What good would it do?"

"People, we've been working together for ten, fifteen, over twenty years some of us." Eddie's voice was rising. "Don't we know what we think by now? Aren't there some values we stand for together? That's what we should talk about. Our common values. What we believe in. Where we think the company should go."

"But those are not our decisions to make!"

"I'm not saying we make the decisions. I'm saying we have a point of view. We're the managers of Zoffner Piano and we have a say."

"It sounds like the union talking. We'll get thrown out on our ear."

"Then why," Nan asked, "does Elena insist on calling us the leadership council, if we're not supposed to have any say?"

"Because she's not her father. She has no idea how to lead the company. She thinks she can fool us, I guess. Leadership council is just a way to put us in our place."

As this discussion was taking place, Elena and Raul were sitting in her office. Their conversation was on the same topic.

"I hate to say this," Elena offered, "because the veteran managers have been the backbone of this company for so long, but all they seem to do is complain to one another. I can't get them to contribute in our meetings."

"Why is that, I wonder?"

"I ask for their input every meeting."

"I know. Maybe it's not enough, just asking. Maybe you need to insist somehow."

"The truth is, Raul, I know what they want. They want to turn back time. They want to forget about the growth and the future of the company and just make pianos like always. I already know all that, and maybe they know I already know, and so they have nothing to say." She shook her head sadly. "And maybe their message is one I don't really want to hear. They sense that, and they feel powerless. How can I change that?"

"By wanting to hear their message?"

Elena nodded. That was an idea she had entertained a time or two. But there was something wrong about it. It would show weakness and just muddy waters that were already pretty cloudy. She felt sure that she needed to set a clear direction for Zoffner. Opening up the whole debate would only make matters worse. Still, how could things get any worse than they were?

"So how do you think I would go about doing that? Wanting to hear them?"

At the next meeting of the leadership council, Elena gave an update on the planning for the digital business. As usual, the veteran managers listened quietly, passively. During the course of this update, Elena read a list of names she said she and Raul had been *thinking about using for the new division. Among them was Zoffner Digital Pianos. When she had finished, she asked for comments, as always, but this time she added: "I want to hear from you. I especially want to hear about anything that concerns you or worries you in what you have heard."*

*Silence. She let it go on for more than the usual two beats. It lengthened and a couple of people stirred uneasily.*

*"I know you have concerns and worries," she said very quietly, "so I think I'll just wait to hear from you."*

*Someone let out a quick laugh. The managers looked around. No one spoke. Elena waited a long minute that seemed much longer. Finally, Eddie spoke up.*

*"I have a concern about the name. Zoffner Digital Pianos. It puts a word in between Zoffner and Piano. Zoffner Piano is who we are. Zoffner Digital Pianos is wrong. Plus, I don't think an electronic instrument is a piano. A piano is a specific instrument with a long history. We are proud of the part we have played in that history. It doesn't include electronic toys."*

*"OK," Elena said, "let's talk."*

## The Emergence of the Second Principle

In the year since she took over for her father, Elena has been slowly developing influence in the company, although it may not be apparent at first. By pushing ahead with her plans (something her authority and power enable her to do), she has been bringing something into being. It is an idea, a plan, that portends a big change in the life of Zoffner Piano. Her idea has a different meaning for her and Raul than it does for Eddie, Nan, and the other veteran managers.

## The Negotiation of Meaning Is
## at the Heart of Interpersonal Influence

By choosing to stay in the organization, the veteran managers are faced with engaging in some way with Elena's idea and with the difference in its meaning for her and them. They could try to avoid such engagement by simply hanging onto their interpretation of the planned new division, or they could try to avoid engagement by letting go of their understanding and adopting Elena's interpretation. Both of these alternatives, however, cause trouble for them. If they keep their interpretation they would seem to be doomed to an obstructionist stance, which would eventually lead them to leave the company; adopting her interpretation, on the other hand, violates their values and threatens to rob their work of the meaning it holds for them. To stay in the Zoffner community, then, implies some *negotiation of the meaning of Elena's idea*. This negotiation of meaning is at the heart of the interpersonal influence principle.

## The Leader's Perspective Is
## the Container for the Negotiation

Notice that this negotiation will take place on the home field, as it were, of Elena herself. It is *Elena's plan* whose meaning is being negotiated. From the perspective of the second principle, influence with respect to meaning is negotiated between the leader, Elena, and the followers, but within a framework that gives priority to the leader's perspective. This priority is how Elena's greater influence is put into practice. Her perspective is the place from which all other perspectives will be viewed. The values of the veteran managers, their concerns and fears, will be interpreted by Elena, shaped and made use of from her point of view. Elena will take them into account, but she will author the account. It will be her understanding of their concerns, her capacity to empathize with them, her valuing of their values that will make up the new, negotiated meaning.

## The Leader's Perspective Is Open to Question and Doubt

This is at once similar to the first principle and significantly different from it. What has not 'changed from the first to the second principle is the priority of the leader's point of view, the leader's values and concerns. What has changed is that the leader's point of view is open to inquiry, open to negotiation, open to change. This openness of the leader's point of view is what makes leadership happen. With the first principle, the dominant leader's point of view, concerns, and values may be questioned and even doubted, and followers can hope to change them; but such questioning and doubting does not make leadership happen. Just the opposite—it impedes leadership from happening, it is counter to leadership. In the second principle, on the other hand, questioning, doubting, negotiating are constitutive of leadership because the give-and-take is how the priority of the leader's perspective is established and the leader's greater influence comes into being. Without some opposing perspective against which a prior perspective is measured, there is no way for a person to gain the greater influence that makes leadership in the second principle happen. And anyone who manages to gain this kind of priority for their point of view in a community becomes able to make leadership happen and gains the ability to accomplish the leadership tasks.

Elena's position as CEO of Zoffner Piano is the cornerstone of the priority of her point of view. The fact that her family owns the company, that Mr. Karl handed it over to her, makes her views the home base from which all other perspectives will be viewed. Similarly, in hierarchical organizations, the authority and power vested in positions creates such a cornerstone of priority. The difference between the first and second principle lies in how this cornerstone is understood in relation to making leadership happen. From the perspective of the first principle, the priority of a perspective granted by a position of authority and power cannot be questioned or negotiated as an aspect of leadership (only as opposition to leadership); whereas from the perspective of the second principle, to make leadership happen, the priority of such a perspective must take into account differing perspectives while remaining prior to those perspectives.

### Parenthetical Comment on Leadership and Management

This may account for the inconclusiveness of the question of the difference between management and leadership. The aspects of management connected to a position of authority, such as the power to hire and fire, evaluate performance, appoint committees, set standards, organize work, and so forth, are also aspects of the priority of perspective granted by the position. So while on one hand something like performance appraisal hardly seems to have anything to do with leadership, causing some to conclude that management and leadership are not the same; on the other hand it is one way that the person with authority gains priority for a perspective, for a set of values. Hence it is one way that the person with authority gains greater influence, and hence it does play a role in leadership from the perspective of the second principle. In a hierarchical community whose members understand leadership primarily from the perspective of the second principle, management and leadership are likely to be thus ambiguously related.

### The Leader Becomes the Repository
### of Differing Perspectives

With the interpersonal influence principle, the leader becomes the repository of the differing perspectives, values, and concerns in the community or organization. The leader takes these differing perspectives into account by putting them in relation to his or her perspective. In this way the leader allows differences in the community or organization to be active in the process of leadership. Think of the mayor of a small town hearing from various citizens: the hardware store owner fearful of a national chain moving in, a conservationist protesting the removal of trees at the site of a new shopping complex, an impoverished mother hoping for a better-paying job, an educator lobbying for more teachers in the local schools, a developer requesting a zoning change. Regardless of personal orientation toward any of these requests, the mayor recognizes the differing values and perspectives from which the requests flow. The decision may ultimately be to work for one request and work against another, but the very act of agreeing and disagreeing means orienting toward differing values and perspectives, establishing some personal relationship with them and holding these differences on behalf of the community.

## Differences Are Aspects of Leadership

Differences in values and perspectives are brought into leadership and become constitutive of leadership. The leader understands and empathizes with the differing perspectives and needs of followers and becomes the holder, the repository of these differences. By allowing the leader to be understood as the repository of differences, the interpersonal influence principle allows difference and disagreement to inform the accomplishment of the leadership tasks. Instead of differences posing a threat to setting direction, gaining commitment, and facing adaptive challenges, they enrich the resources that can be brought to bear. By retaining the distinction between leader and follower and by understanding the leader to have more influence than followers, the principle allows the leader to accomplish the leadership tasks in contexts of difference and disagreement. For all the dominance of the leader in the first principle, this is not a power the leader possesses. From the perspective of the first principle, difference and disagreement impede the accomplishment of the leadership tasks. This limitation is overcome by the second principle.

*Elena's invitation to Eddie and the other managers—"let's talk"—
marked a crucial letting go of the first principle for both Elena and
Eddie, and in time, for everyone. What was being let go was the idea
that Elena should or could create leadership and be responsible for
leadership on her own, without some engagement and responsibility
on the part of followers. Elena felt this from that day forward every
time she had ideas about the business, whether about strategy or the
most mundane details. At first she felt a sense of having lost something: autonomy, control, self-reliance, power.*

*"I can't even think about turning around without thinking about
how it will affect key functions," she confided to Raul. "Everything
is so much harder."*

*As far as Eddie and some of the other veteran managers were
concerned, they too felt a sense of loss.*

*"Like losing your innocence in a way," Eddie said to Nan. "I can
never just think about doing my job well and letting Mr. Karl sweat
the big stuff like I used to. I feel like I have to think about strategy too.
And about other parts of the business. I have to develop a point of
view that represents the values and needs of manufacturing. That's
what Mr. Karl used to do. I realize now that he developed that point
of view and somehow he was always right. His point of view was
manufacturing's point of view. How did he do that? Elena can't do
that and so I have to. But I'm not Mr. Karl either. How do I do it?"*

*So in some ways it seemed to Elena and to others on the leadership
council that things just kept getting worse, harder, slower, less clear, more
of a burden. They worked longer hours, with more argument, hurt feelings, anger, compromise, uncertainty. But there were some ways, hard
to see at first, in which something was being gained. For Elena it was
gradually dawning on her that she was gaining an ability to lead.*

*"I always thought there were only two ways to be a leader. Either you were born a leader or you learned how to be a leader," she told Raul. "I never realized that you could become a leader by thinking differently about leadership itself. I used to think that I wasn't a leader and wasn't likely to learn how to be one—I knew I could never be like my father. But this whole leadership council thing, even though it started out being just some words, is changing the way I think about leadership. It's not all about me and what I am or what I can learn. It's not just what I do that counts, it's what I do with followers that counts. So even though that makes me feel constrained and like I've lost power, in another way I've freed myself to become the leader and I've gained power."*

Eddie, too, was beginning to recognize that in what was being lost, things were being gained. He and Nan often had the same reactions.

*"I know what you mean,"* Nan once said, *"about feeling responsible for more of the business. I have more trouble sleeping since I started taking myself seriously as a member of the leadership council. Things I used to leave to Mr. Karl and never thought about, they bother me now. It's like I'm waking up to the fact that Zoffner is about more than the balance sheets. The balance sheets are connected to things like the strategy, the new product line, employee attitudes. The pieces are starting to fit together somehow. And I see things Elena doesn't see. I see things differently than she does. I would make different decisions than she does."*

*"Right,"* Eddie responded. *"Just the kind of thoughts I always kept to myself before. Not with Mr. Karl, because I hardly ever disagreed with him, but early on with Elena. I disagreed with just about everything she said or did, and I still do. Only now disagreeing is part of what she expects of me. It's funny. I'm supposed to*

*make my disagreements known so we can talk things out. Sometimes she even changes her mind when I disagree, and I feel like I'm making a difference, but then I think 'Do I want to make that kind of a difference?' I feel like I have to really be careful now about what I disagree on. You know, be careful what you wish for, you just may get it!"*

## The Second Principle and the Leadership Tasks

Now that the second principle is beginning to emerge at Zoffner Piano, how will the leadership tasks be accomplished? What changes in the way people talk to one another, the context of their interactions, the content of their discussions, the understanding of their roles and responsibilities will be evident in the organization as leadership is gradually re-viewed from the perspective afforded by the principle of interpersonal influence?

### Setting Direction

Remember that from the perspective of the first principle direction is set by the leader, who, through an understanding shared within the community or organization, possesses personal qualities and abilities that enable the chosen direction to compel belief within the community. It is this shared understanding that allowed Mr. Karl to nearly always be right in Eddie's eyes, so that Eddie hardly ever disagreed with him. But from the understanding of leadership afforded by the second principle, the possession of these kinds of personal qualities, however desirable they may otherwise be, does not guarantee that followers will believe in the rightness of the leader's vision. The knowledge of the right direction, the achievement of a vision, is not granted simply because a person possesses leadership ability. Instead, the leader must work for knowledge and vision and gains it in time only by taking into account the differing perspectives and concerns of followers. Although, as with the first principle, direction is finally understood as a vision seen through the leader's eyes, vision as understood from the perspective of the second principle is effective only to the extent that those eyes see their vision within a frame that includes the perspectives and concerns of followers. Followers are not influenced by the leader's vision unless they can see the part they have played in creating that vision.

Part of the reason that Elena is gaining influence with Eddie, even though he still mostly disagrees with her, is that he is sensing his own responsibility for the positions he takes, the values he espouses. The vision retains its characteristic as coming from Elena as the leader, but it is understood that she is re-presenting (presenting again) perspectives and values that may differ from her own. Notice that, in this analysis, the second principle could make sense of a wide range of leadership styles, from deciding alone after consulting with followers to active participation of followers in decisions.

We saw that one limitation of the dominance principle is encountered when the complexity of the community's context increases and the decisions of the leader with respect to direction are consequently poorer; the leader's ability as a leader is called into question, limiting the power of the first principle to make leadership happen. Because the second principle is itself more complex (by virtue of its inclusion of multiple perspectives in the leader's vision), increased complexity can be more easily addressed. Ambiguous or confusing circumstances can be viewed from a variety of perspectives.

In addition, when the leader's decisions with respect to direction do not turn out well, it need not become a crisis of leadership itself. Because a wider range of possible choices with respect to direction are brought to bear, the possibility of ambiguity with respect to direction is admitted into the understanding of leadership. Such ambiguity, in turn, tends to ameliorate criticism of the leader, because the leader is viewed as necessarily taking into account differing viewpoints within the community. Although the leader might be blamed for a poor decision, the recognition that the decision took into account some degree of empathy with differing values and perspectives within the community means that followers assume some degree of responsibility for decisions. A leader might still lose credibility, but less because of a failure to dominate the situation (as in the first principle) and more because of a failure to negotiate and integrate the many differences within the community.

## Creating Commitment

If the essential logic of commitment in the first principle is loyalty to the leader, the essential logic of commitment in the interpersonal influence principle is participation in the leader's integrating perspective. In other words, commitment in the second principle is created as one's own interests, perspectives, and values are accounted for in the actions and decisions of the leader. When Eddie disagrees and Elena takes notice, Eddie becomes more committed to Elena's perspective because he sees his perspective reflected there. ("Be careful what you wish for," as he says.) As Nan sees how her job of working with the balance sheets is connected to things such as strategy, she becomes more committed to Elena's strategy, because she sees her work reflected there even when she would "make different decisions" than Elena does.

From the understanding afforded by the second principle, commitment means investing in a leader's perspective because you have in some way informed that perspective, whether you agree with the perspective or not. Remember that the limit of the first principle with respect to maintaining commitment tends to be reached when the leader fails personally to live up to the loyalty of followers and that when this happens, commitment to the community or organization overall is threatened. Thus, for example, a leader who violates the mores and norms of the community begins to lose the sense of being the leader, and leadership—the ability to accomplish the leadership tasks—begins to be lost. The second principle provides a mechanism by which followers can disagree with and even disapprove of the views or actions of the leader without threatening a loss of leadership. In other words, followers have some latitude to influence the leader and also to criticize and even censure the leader without necessarily having the leader lose the greater degree of influence in the community that is required for leadership. Again we see how the logic is more complex in the second principle: complex and incompatible judgments of the leader are possible without breaking down the leader's greater influence in the relationship. And we also see how this greater complexity makes the second principle more difficult to enact. The leader's actions and decisions can be seen as not integrating competing perspectives and values; followers can lose their ability to be influenced by the leader when they feel left out; difficult discussions aimed at integrating differing views can leave the leader and followers less aligned with one another, less committed to continuing to work together.

If commitment in the first principle can be called loyalty, commitment in the second principle is *alignment*. Commitment is not a matter, as in the first principle, of there being a leader to commit to and be loyal to; rather it is the outcome of a continuing set of negotiations that continue to come out on balance in favor of a leader who is creating more influence than followers. Followers who "get influenced" and whose attempts at influence are subordinated to the greater influence of the leader come into alignment with the leader because they have participated in a dynamic interaction, because their views have been taken into the leader's views in some way, because the leader's own views have been reconsidered in light of followers' views. The very things that tend to threaten commitment and loyalty in the first principle—disagreement, difference, clashing values—are reconstituted in the second principle into an exchange of influence essential for the creation of commitment and alignment.

### Facing Adaptive Challenge

How will the community deal with internal and external threats? The task of facing challenges is the responsibility of the leader in the logic of the first principle. Under the personal dominance principle, the leader faces challenges on behalf of the community; it is the leader who must recognize the challenge and the leader who is required to frame the response. The second principle, because it enables leadership to be understood as a dynamic interaction between leader and followers, allows challenges to be recognized and responses to be framed from multiple points of view. No longer is the community or organization limited to the unitary point of view of the leader in recognizing and responding to challenges. An example of the use of multiple viewpoints to recognize and respond to challenges can be seen in the dynamics of multifunctional senior manager groups. For example, the marketing director applies frameworks of market analysis to recognize a shift in markets away from the organization's leading product, the production manager sees the organization's main product lagging in technological advancements, the sales director sees a decline in orders in certain geographical areas, and so forth. These multiple viewpoints can be synthesized to create a complex picture of what is happening. A response can be framed that takes into account the various frameworks for understanding the challenge—focus groups can help the organization understand customer needs, new technology can be adopted, sales approaches can be modified. The role of the leader in this process is to act as the integrating force, and to accomplish this, the leader takes a perspective that is inclusive of the various functional frameworks.

This inclusive framework may have a bias toward one or another of the functional frameworks because the leader may have a background in one of them, but the leader's framework is nonetheless understood to integrate the others because leadership in the interpersonal influence principle makes sense when the leader has more influence than the followers. Someone, in other words, has to break the ties and resolve any conflicts that arise among the various frameworks so that a unified set of actions to address the challenge can be taken.

We saw that the personal dominance principle encounters a limit to its effectiveness with respect to facing challenges when a challenge unrecognized by the leader cannot be addressed by the community or organization. Such a challenge might spell disaster for the community. The second principle redresses this limitation by creating multiple opportunities and multiple points of view by which a challenge can be recognized. The second principle is in this way an advance over the first principle and is also more complex; and again, this increased complexity is both an advantage and a difficulty. It is advantageous to be able to frame challenges from multiple viewpoints, but it is also more difficult to enact speedy and decisive actions in response to challenges. Where the first principle was capable of producing swift action as the leader responded unitarily, the second principle, as it works through its dynamic interaction between leader and followers, often produces slower and less decisive action because differing ways of framing action are being brought to bear.

## Review of the Limits of the First and Capacities of the Second Principle

Let's recall the limits of the first principle and summarize the capacities of the interpersonal influence principle, which overcome these limitations and form the essential logic of the second principle. Table 3.1 lays out the factors involved.

This helps us understand the second principle as an adaptation to the limits of the first principle and an attempt to transcend those limits. In adapting to these limits and transcending them, people do not want to lose the capacities of the first principle unnecessarily, and so whenever possible the second principle holds onto what is still useful about the first principle. For example, the idea that the balance of influence between the leader and followers favors the leader—that the leader influences followers more than followers influence the leader—retains a key aspect of the first principle: the leader is still held responsible for leadership and held accountable for the effectiveness of leadership. In effect, interpersonal influence is a way of keeping the leader at the center of leadership, responsible and

**Table 3.1  Limits of the First Principle and the Corresponding Capacities of the Second Principle**

| Tasks | Limits of First Principle | Capacities of Second Principle |
|---|---|---|
| Setting direction | When the complexity of the context makes the leader's decisions unclear or ambiguous, the leader loses legitimacy. | Ambiguity can be understood as an aspect of the situation, not just the result of the leader's decisions. |
| Creating commitment | When the leader behaves in ways that fail to maintain the loyalty of followers, commitment is threatened. | Commitment is understood to be to a perspective shared in a community, not given to the leader personally. |
| Facing adaptive challenge | Challenges unrecognized by the leader cannot be addressed by the community or organization. | More challenges can be recognized and addressed because multiple perspectives are enabled; the climate for innovation can improve. |

accountable, while increasing the capacity of leadership to operate in more complex contexts of multiple perspectives and values. The second principle is thus a remarkable achievement. It addresses limitations in the first principle's capacity to carry out the leadership tasks while building on the capacities of the first principle.

If my intuition is useful here, the emergence of the second principle as a way of understanding leadership occurred slowly over a period of a century or more from about the early eighteenth century into the nineteenth, during the Enlightenment and the rise of democracy. (Remember this is not a claim that interpersonal influence itself arose in this time—it has, of course, been around as long as humans have—only that interpersonal influence came in this time to be understood as an approach to *leadership*.) All that time, of course, the personal dominance principle was still available for use in contexts where it was effective (as well as in contexts where it was not). The first principle does not go away: it cannot do so because it is at the heart of the very idea of leadership, and so long as humans need to accomplish leadership tasks (as framed here or as otherwise framed) the first principle will find a place in human interactions, even if only in a form as reorganized and re-viewed by the second principle.

It is important to review and recognize the achievement of the second principle before we try to understand what its limitations might be. The principle moves from a personal understanding of leadership to an interpersonal understanding. This seemingly simple change in the way leadership is understood has been profound in its effects. In the logic of the second principle, leadership is understood as happening not when the leader *acts on* but when a person in the leadership role *acts with* followers. In this way followers become integral to leadership.

The second principle interprets the leader as a member of the community with special duties and responsibilities, subject to the same rules and expectations as other members. The second principle constructs the values, perspectives, and motives of the leader as standing in relation to the values, perspectives, and motives of followers. This enables the emergence of productive disagreement and conflict in a community without raising the specter of disloyalty to the leader or subversion of the leader's power.

In general terms, the first principle affords an understanding of the leader as the *source* of leadership, in which the followers receive it from the leader. The second principle affords an understanding that it is the interaction between the leader and followers that is the source of leadership, with the leader as the *repository* of leadership, who re-presents it, articulates it, enacts it within the community or organization.

We see here again what we saw with respect to personal dominance: our cultural proclivity for seeing the world from the point of view of the individual predisposes us to miss the way that leadership, all leadership, is the shared achievement of a community. We saw how the personal dominance principle, though it creates an understanding of leadership as an almost completely individual achievement, must itself be shared within a community for such leadership to take hold and work. The same is again true for the second principle. Although the sense it makes of leadership is still basically individual (while moving toward more inclusion of followers), the principle itself must be a shared resource in the community. No matter what version of leadership we could imagine, from the most intensely individualistic to the most completely distributed and consensual, lying under all forms there must be some shared principle that makes leadership make sense, that provides the meaning of leadership. And this underlying shared principle is brought into being, nurtured, enacted, trusted, taken for granted, and sometimes even found wanting *by a whole community of people*. From this point of view, the difference between a leader and followers comes down to a difference in ways of participating in a shared understanding. Shared leadership is not a *kind* of leadership; all leadership *is* shared leadership.

# Chapter Four

# The Limits of Interpersonal Influence

*Under Elena's leadership, Raul, Eddie, Nan, and the other managers of the Zoffner leadership council accomplished the leadership tasks together for a number of years after the retirement of Mr. Karl. He didn't even visit the offices or the plant much anymore, preferring to spend most of his time fly-fishing up in the mountains.*

*He probably wouldn't have recognized things anyway, because much had changed during those years. Although Elena was firmly established as the leader, both because of her authority and because of her capacity to encompass the various perspectives within the company, the managers did not look to her for the kind of leadership they had once looked to Mr. Karl for. The other managers had come to understand that leadership was partly their responsibility as well as Elena's. It was their responsibility to bring alternative views and conflicts out in the open where they could be productively negotiated among all of them. They had become much more skilled at discussing and negotiating such differences and often were able to arrive at effective decisions as a group. They had also grown confident that when these alternatives, differences, and conflicts became hard or impossible to resolve, Elena would be able to integrate and resolve them within their shared process in the leadership council. For her part, Elena had learned how to nurture these useful discussions and negotiations, developing a keen sense of just when her integrating* point of view was required. She knew that if she spoke up too soon, she would be seen as too dominant, whereas if she waited too long, she would be seen as too passive and not playing her proper role in the leadership process. It was a balancing act she had grown comfortable with.

Where the business was concerned, things had grown more complex, more difficult, and more urgent in the past few months. Soon after the plant was built for making digital instruments, Elena and the leadership council decided that the best course was to separate the two parts of the company into distinct divisions. They created a corporate entity called Zoffner Music, with Elena as CEO, to handle some centralized functions such as human resources, legal, and finance, and to oversee and coordinate the two divisions. The old-line business retained its original name and identity, Zoffner Piano Company. The new digital keyboard business they called Musitron.

After an initial burst of success that some attributed to its connection to Zoffner, Musitron began to struggle. For the past three years, the fledgling division's revenue had dwindled and at the same time R&D costs continued to grow. No matter what new bells and whistles the designers and engineers came up with, Musitron was finding it increasingly difficult to compete with the established names in the digital keyboard business.

Zoffner Piano Company was called on to support Musitron. Profits from the traditional business were poured into the start-up. This was, of course, creating a squeeze in the traditional business. With the increasing cost of materials combined with their long-term strategy of keeping their instruments affordable, Zoffner Piano's margins were dwindling, and losing revenue to Musitron was just making matters worse.

To top it off, the two companies—Zoffner Piano under Eddie and Musitron under Raul—had developed completely different and incompatible cultures. Although they occupied adjacent parcels of land, the people of one division hardly ever came into contact with those of the other. This wasn't surprising. They had almost nothing in common.

Most Zoffner Piano employees were over fifty years old and were devoted craftsmen who spent every day dealing with physical entities: wood, iron, drawn wire. These they fashioned with their hands into the delicate and sensitive mechanisms that formed a piano. Musitron employees, on the other hand, were likely to be under thirty-five, electrical or computer engineers who spent most of the day dealing with ideas, diagrams, flow charts, and computer programs. The instrument itself—the physical keyboard—was nothing more to most of these engineers than a box to hold the digital technology, and there was even talk of contracting for production of the keyboards with a manufacturer who could do it cheaper.

Musitron people tended to laugh when they heard that Zoffner people thought of them as gear-heads who made toys; they knew that digital technology was the future of musical instruments. Zoffner people tended to cringe when they heard that the Musitron people referred to the beautiful instruments of wood, iron, and strings as "analog pianos."

In the past year, Raul and Eddie, who had for a time worked well together, began to show the strain of this culture clash. In meetings of the leadership council, their differences were becoming more pronounced and more strident. It was getting harder and harder for Elena to encompass such a divergence of worldviews, and for the past month she had been pushing and prodding in the meetings.

*"We have got to find a way out of this,"* she said one day. *"We're starting to pull against one another and it's tearing us apart. I can't keep trying to be in the middle. There is no damn middle anymore, we've grown so far apart. Does anybody have an idea?"*

No one spoke for a time. Finally Raul said, *"One of my engineers has been noodling with an idea for combining some aspects of digital technology with the traditional piano. It's just some ideas at this point, but looks promising. What if we collaborated to come up with a completely new product?"*

This was something Raul had mentioned to Elena before in private, but here it was out in the open in the leadership council. She waited, not saying anything, wanting to hear how Eddie would respond.

*"I don't know,"* he began. *"I'm doubtful because of the differences in culture. How could it ever work? At the same time, I realize we're up against some hard times if we don't do something bold. I'm willing to talk about it. See what we can come up with, I guess."*

*"OK,"* said Elena, *"I suggest we get a team together to look at feasibility."*

*"A cross-divisional team,"* said Raul.

*"Of course,"* Elena said and turned to Eddie.

He nodded his head and smiled uncertainly.

*"Who's in charge of the team?"* he asked.

Everyone on the council looked around. The truth struck them suddenly. Nan gave it voice: *"We can't put anyone in charge of the team, because the person would have to come from one of the divisions. The two divisions have to be on an equal footing if this is going to work."*

*"So it's a self-managed team. They report to the leadership council,"* Elena said.

*That was the beginning of another changing of their minds about leadership. And it would finally result in an outcome not a single one of them expected that day.*

## Limits on the Second Principle's Capacity to Make Sense of Leadership

At the end of Chapter Two, I proposed that the taken-for-granted truths organized by the first principle have built-in limits. Such limits are encountered in certain contexts where leadership cannot be recognized—cannot be understood as happening—when interpreted according to the truths of the principle. I asserted that the second principle, interpersonal influence, arises (in our Western culture) as a way of overcoming the limits of the first principle. It is this second principle that Elena and the managers (and in time most of the employees) of Zoffner Music have constructed for their use in re-creating leadership after Mr. Karl's retirement. (Their move from the first to the second principle was, I suggest, an example of leadership development—not because the second principle is in some absolute way better than the first, but because the first principle had reached its limits and another, more complex, principle was required in a new context to bring back the possibility of leadership.)

Just as the first principle contains its own limitations, so does the second principle. The contexts limiting the first principle included loss of the leader, loss of followers, the development of independence by followers, recognition of limits by the leader, increases in contextual complexity beyond the capacity of the leader to encompass, a personal failure of the leader to embody the ideals of the community or organization, and the emergence of challenges that the leader could not recognize, frame, or articulate. The multiple perspectives brought to bear by the second principle, along with the integration of those perspectives by the leader, helped overcome these limits of the first principle while retaining the useful distinction (in our Western culture) between leader and follower. Are there contexts in our world today that are pushing even this highly useful second principle toward its limits? What are those contexts? What limits does the second principle bring with it? What hope lies beyond the second principle for overcoming those limits? These are the questions that will occupy the rest of this book.

We saw that the limits of the first principle were, in accord with the nature of the taken-for-granted truths that principle organizes, often personal in nature. It is in the very capacity to make sense that a knowledge principle also encounters its limits of making sense. Because the second principle makes sense of leadership as a negotiation of influence among more or less autonomous individuals with the leader acting as a repository and integrator of differing perspectives and values, it is within these capacities that we will be likely to find the limits of interpersonal influence. What contexts of life in our world today might be pushing the second principle toward its limits? In other words, what kinds of things are happening that tend to result in the loss of leadership, not just when based on personal dominance but when based on interpersonal influence as well?

### Unity Embracing Diversity

To answer this question we can begin with some of the most-discussed changes in life in the last century. The advent of global transportation, instant worldwide communication, and a growing recognition of the interdependence of economies are bringing about a world in which the main challenge is to create unity embracing diversity. I understand this to mean that outcomes common to all (which may include shared goals but are not limited to them) and affecting all need to account for diverse worldviews as if those differing worldviews were equally valid, with no one worldview being understood as the controlling view. Thus the worldview of the Palestinians and the worldview of the Israelis at the time of this writing—though each worldview opposes the very existence of the other—are challenged in the emerging world to embrace one another without honoring one at the expense of the other in order to reach the "final status" talks on the future of those worldviews. As I write this, one of the very sticking points is the Israeli insistence that their worldview—their sense of reality in the region—be the controlling view. Even though the second principle affords a way to make sense of difference and conflict in a leader-follower context, whenever there is a need for leadership in other than leader-follower contexts and where differing (and sometimes conflicting) worldviews are being put forward as equally warrantable, a formidable challenge is presented to the sensemaking power of the interpersonal influence principle. The second principle depends on the greater influence of one point of view (the leader's) with respect to followers. In effect the second principle depends on the distinction between the leader's control of worldviews and the resulting power to integrate differences into a unity, and the followers' need to have differences so integrated and their resulting willingness to have their worldviews relativized to that of the leader.

A more incisive example of this kind of limiting context with respect to the second principle came about as a result of the calamity of EgyptAir Flight 990, which crashed after taking off from John F. Kennedy Airport in New York on October 31, 1999. Because the flight departed from an American city and involved an Egyptian airliner, both American and Egyptian crash investigators became involved in the investigation. Everyone, both Egyptian and U.S. officials, seemed to agree that the task was to determine what really happened on that ill-fated flight. An Egyptian official quoted in the *New York Times* (November 22, 1999) declared that the team was on a "joint search for the truth." Yet, given the equal footing on which the differing cultures were being placed, was this an achievable goal? Looking at the facts from two different-but-equal points of view, could the team ever fully agree on "what happened," much less on "the truth"? Recall that the critical issue in this crash seemed to be the meaning of words uttered by the copilot, who was flying the plane alone when it began to lose altitude. Was he praying to

God as a prelude to committing suicide, or was he just praying to God? Wouldn't there always be some irreducible difference in the U.S. Judeo-Christian and the Egyptian Islamic interpretations of the copilot's words on the cockpit voice recorder? How could this difference be resolved into a single version of the truth without asserting the ultimacy of one of the worldviews? Wouldn't this matter always be equivocal, the truth depending on the view one took? Without a leader—either in person or in the form of a controlling worldview—it would seem that no "joint search for the truth" could ever be successful, simply because there is no joint truth.

Thus, as the second principle is applied to the context of the Egyptian-U.S. team, it is hard, if not impossible, to make sense of what was happening as being leadership. Just the opposite: leadership seemed to be missing. By the logic of the second principle, someone or some worldview would need to take precedence over the other for any leadership to happen. This lack of leadership (as interpreted from the perspective afforded by interpersonal influence) could have been understood by some people as the problem in the team's shared work. I am proposing another way to understand the challenge of their shared work: they were using a leadership principle that was too limited to make sense of the context they faced, and thus the leadership tasks could not be effectively performed.

### Limiting Contexts in American Communities

These kinds of challenges to the sensemaking capacity of the second principle are not limited to cross-cultural, cross-national contexts. Limitations to the sensemaking capacity of the influence principle are being encountered in American communities, where there has been a slow movement toward recognition of the legitimacy of differing voices in community life. More and more, voices that have been silenced in the past are being invited, however haltingly, into conversations on community life: jobs, schools, transportation, economic development, the environment, the arts, public health and safety. All of these issues, which used to be decided on by small groups of insiders sharing a more-or-less homogeneous set of perspectives and values, are being gradually opened up to a diversity of perspectives and values. As this happens, formerly powerless voices and formerly privileged voices are searching for a way to understand their participation in such conversations.

Those who have in the past been without voice and power and who are now seeking and ostensibly being afforded "a place at the table" can find it difficult to understand how such a change will work. Even when the existing structure of power and influence in the community is open to change, how can those who have been marginal for so long ever gain enough influence to lead? Leadership would require that they somehow become a source of more influence in the community than the traditionally privileged sources. The second principle's way of understanding leadership as a greater flow of influence from leader to follower tends to restrict people and groups that have not had influence in the past to one of two stances: joining with the existing sources of influence in the hopes of eventually winning enough relative influence to make a difference or entering into conflict with the traditional sources of influence to more forcefully win a larger share of influence. Other possibilities—dialogue, for example—are not understood from the logic of the second principle to constitute leadership and thus are disqualified from consideration as ways of creating leadership.

At the same time, the traditionally privileged voices in some communities are searching for ways to share leadership, to grant some influence to others, without losing their own power and influence. The conundrum is how to carve out a piece of influence large enough to grant some legitimacy to traditionally marginalized people, usually representing a minority of some kind within the community, without giving up leadership to these voices. The justification is that the representatives of the majority, presumably the traditional leaders of the community, are the source of greater influence and thus should rightfully be the source of leadership. From this perspective, the move to share leadership is an attempt to open up leadership to the influence of followers in accord with the concept of effectiveness derived from the second principle, but this opening up must not go too far or it becomes an abrogation of leadership and by extension of the responsibility to lead.

From the perspective of the traditionally marginalized community members, being included in leadership but only as followers (only as people with less influence than the leaders) is half a loaf at best. To enter into the life of the community fully means being able to exercise leadership in the community, which means somehow having more influence than the traditional leaders, the very situation that the traditional leaders feel it is their responsibility to avoid. Thus even in communities where, with the best of intentions, people are attempting to right historical inequities and share leadership, the context is one of a mutually unproductive search for leadership in which the traditional leaders are often cast as repressing the marginal voice and in which the marginalized groups are cast as causing trouble and demanding more than they have a right to expect.

This mutually unproductive search for leadership in many communities is thus a context pushing the interpersonal influence principle to the limit of its capacity to make sense of leadership. The interaction between the traditionally disempowered and the traditionally honored cannot be understood as accomplishing leadership tasks with the assumption that either will "influence the other more than be influenced by the other." Neither participant in such a process is willing to understand being influenced more by the other as leadership. Depending on the point of view, it is either subjugation or abrogation, but not leadership. This is a fundamental challenge to the capacity of the interpersonal influence principle to make leadership happen.

### Limiting Contexts in Organizations

The limits of influence are also being encountered in some organizations, often those facing rapid and unexpected changes in technology and markets. These organizations open up to closer relationships with all kinds of constituents including suppliers and customers, cross-functional work becomes more prevalent, the hierarchy is flattened as work is organized closer to the operations level, senior-manager groups seek to work in greater recognition of their interdependence, organizations take in a greater diversity of people in their workforces and markets, and attempts are made to leverage knowledge across the enterprise. Each of these represents a strong challenge to the capacity of the interpersonal influence principle to make sense of leadership tasks.

***Collaborative Relationships with Suppliers and Customers.***  Organizations are seeking to form collaborative, partner relationships with constituents traditionally thought of as being outside the organization, such as customers, suppliers, unions, even competitors. The organization is in this way being viewed less as a self-contained, closed system and more as an interacting, open system. As is the case with increasing diversity, this often means that the differing values, perspectives, and needs of these constituents are becoming more than factors to be accounted for in organizational plans and are becoming integrated aspects of those plans. For example, an automobile manufacturer that in the past issued specifications to a supplier for, say, windshields, is now seeking ways for its engineers to work directly with engineers from the supplier to jointly design the windshields in an effort to improve safety and lower costs. This effort is challenging because of the differing cultures of the two companies arising from different values and perspectives and sometimes clashing priorities. To make a person from either of the collaborating organizations the leader of such a team might cause more problems than it would solve, as the managers on the Zoffner leadership council have foreseen. How are the leadership tasks of such a cross-organizational (or cross-divisional) team to be performed? There is obvious value in approaching work as if it were shared between and among differing communities, but on the other hand, there is also a profound challenge embedded in it. If the second principle fails to make sense of leadership in such a context, any failure of the team to perform effectively may be due as much to this as to other factors, such as clashing culture, jealousy, or infighting.

*Cross-Functional Teams.* Even when collaborating teams are from within the same community or organization, and presumably share many aspects of the same culture, they feel the leadership challenge when they are constituted on a cross-functional basis. For example, suppose a cross-functional team created to develop a new product includes people from R&D (where the product was conceived), marketing (where the product's fit with the company's markets is in question), production (where there are concerns about the effect of the new product on manufacturing processes), legal (where the new product is setting off alarm bells because of possible liability issues), and sales (where the product is seen as the next great offering that will win back eroding revenues). If the organization, as is happening more and more often, thinks of the shared work of this cross-functional team as largely determining whether and how and what to invest in this new product, how will the leadership tasks be performed? Does the second principle, with its logic of a leader as the repository of shared meaning who has greater influence than followers, provide a way to make sense of leadership in this context? Who would "lead" such a team? Someone from one of the functions represented on the team? Someone from a higher level? And if so, in what sense is the team being given responsibility for its work? Again, the second principle may encounter severe limits in this context.

## Organizing Around Work

Making cross-functional teams more directly responsible for outcomes is a specific example of a more general move toward organizing around the work and pushing decision making closer to the operational level and, in the process, flattening the hierarchy and making people throughout the organization more directly responsible for their work. As operational employees take responsibility for making decisions in direct communication with customers, for example, they may do so within broad frameworks laid down by higher levels of management. Broad frameworks for actions and decisions may turn out to be qualitatively different from standard operating procedures and work protocols, not merely different in degree as many may suppose. Since even the strictest work routines are open to local interpretation, broad frameworks within a significantly flattened structure may allow the development of semi-autonomous communities of excellence around specific areas of work. Such communities may be able to deliver significantly higher-quality outcomes for organizational constituents, but how might the leadership tasks of the larger organization then be accomplished? How could leadership in such a context be understood? Can the principle of interpersonal influence make adequate sense of such a context?

### Changing Nature of Senior-Level Management Work

One of the outcomes of creating an organization in which the various functions are expected to work more interdependently and in which employees are expected to take more direct responsibility for their work within broad frameworks is a change in the nature of work in senior-level management groups. In traditional organizations, each member of the senior team is responsible for the co-ordination and control of a function with the others; the senior team is, in effect, the location of coordination "from above"—in other words, from a level of more abstraction—the classic bureaucratic hierarchy. As coordination begins to happen more horizontally from work group to work group instead of from senior manager to senior manager, the work of the senior group changes. Instead of spending most of their time reporting to one another on what is happening within each function (a classic operations review, for example), the senior team as a whole must engage in interdependent work. If the marketing teams and the production

teams are increasingly talking to one another and working together across their differing functions, the marketing manager and
production manager must also learn to understand each other's
work and worldview. Again, we see how differing values and perspectives are arriving at the table on more equal footing. The central sensemaking capacities of the second principle begin to falter
when a higher-level manager can no longer break the tie between
marketing and production, when some outcome other than integration from a higher and "more influential" perspective is being
called forth.

## Increasing Diversity in Organizations

As diversity increases in organizations it also creates a challenge to
the sensemaking power of the second principle. If our organizations
are going to embrace differing cultures and whole differing worldviews, they will need to be able to embrace differing values, philosophies, attitudes, ideas, feelings, and meanings all at once. They
must not see one worldview as being contained within or nurtured
by another, but rather see differing worldviews as mutually sustaining. When differing and sometimes even antagonistic worldviews
are put into a mutually sustaining relationship the result may be
ambiguous, equivocal, conflicted, unresolved. Unity embracing
diversity would seem in principle unable to produce an unequivocal point of view. The very meaning of such seemingly unifying and
integrating ideas as vision, decision, and solution may be changing.
Ambiguity and multiple meanings are likely to become more and
more common in our experience in organizations, and this may not
be something to fear but something to work with and even to benefit from. The move toward diversity, then, poses impressive limits
on our ability to understand leadership as interpersonal influence.
After all, any human being is necessarily limited to some perspective or another. In becoming the repository of meanings under the
second principle, a leader must integrate multiple meanings and in
the process raise some above others—which is precisely what be-

comes impossible when multiple meanings have equal claim on the organization.

### The Learning Organization and Knowledge Management

Finally, the whole set of ideas implicit in what is being called the *learning organization* form a challenge to the sensemaking power of the second principle. The notion that knowledge in one part of the organization can be transferred usefully to another part, that the organization as a whole can learn from the collective experiences of its members, calls forth a more complex context in which leadership tasks will be performed. It is a context characterized by people learning from others who have different approaches and different values in relation to the organization's work—design engineers learning from the experience of line operators, sales managers in the U.S. learning from salespeople in Malaysia, research scientists learning from marketing professionals. It is a context in which the idea of relatively stable organizational functions is replaced by the idea of flowing and interconnected work, in which definable jobs have been replaced by interdependent tasks. It is a context in which the idea of relative stability and planned change is replaced by that of continuous adaptation, an ongoing process of changing the changes. It is a context in which an organization adapts as a part of a larger system that includes what used to be thought of as the "external" environment, which calls into question the value of annual or other time-specific planning cycles.

## Writing About These New Contexts

The emergence of these challenging new contexts in organizations is mirrored in the work of a number of writers on leadership who reflect the limitations of the interpersonal influence principle. In *Leadership for the Twenty-First Century* (1991), for example, Joseph Rost discusses leadership as a process shared equally between leader and followers. Ronald Heifetz, writing in *Leadership Without Easy*

*Answers* (1994) describes leadership as the process of making adaptive changes that require people to examine and redefine basic assumptions. He points out that existing ideas of leadership are too often confused with ideas about authority and hence tied to the person of the authority figure, who is seldom in a position to ring in the kind of adaptive changes leadership requires. Writing about the need to change ideas of leadership in the schools, Linda Lambert and her associates in *The Constructivist Leader* (1995) define leadership in terms of "reciprocal processes" between leaders and followers. In his seminal work, *Sensemaking in Organizations* (1995), Karl Weick emphasizes the importance of organizational and social processes that involve the interconnections of work and the mutual interpretations of events people make in creating organizational action. These ideas all implicitly challenge the basic logic of the second principle that leaders are the integrating repositories of differing perspectives and values who influence followers more than followers influence them.

## Summary of Limiting Contexts

Before returning to the story of Zoffner to look in on how one community has struggled with the limits of the second principle, let me try to summarize in broader terms what I propose are the contexts limiting the capacity of the second principle.

The most striking and perhaps most general context is the increasing mutual acknowledgment of shared work between and among people and communities holding significantly differing worldviews, values, cultures. This is an aspect of globalization of economies, communication, and transportation; honoring diversity (recognizing differences from one's own worldview as being legitimate in their own right, not deficits); the increase in open-systems thinking in communities and organizations; and the move in many organizations to structure work around the needs and values of customers, clients, and other end users, which almost always results in the breakdown of differentiating internal structures and the discovery of the interdependence of differing functions.

Recognizing shared work in such contexts leads to the need to accomplish the leadership tasks across differing worldviews. This results in a paradox. Goals and visions cannot be univocally articulated, and yet, are not goals and visions by nature supposed to be unifying? Commitment cannot be to a leader or to a unified community, and yet, is not leadership supposed to be about creating such unifying commitment? An adaptive challenge cannot be articulated in terms that everyone can agree to or even understand. The exact nature of "the challenge facing us" is open to multiple interpretations.

The differing worldviews cannot be embraced by any one of the worldviews. Each worldview is understood to be self-generating, autonomous, self-justifying. The only hope would seem to be finding areas of agreement across differing worldviews that do not require any one of them to give up the sources of its internal logic and integrity.

The leadership tasks cannot be accomplished through negotiation of influence. There is little if any basis for mutual influence. The worldviews are understood to be unmoved with respect to one another. And since any person must be a participant in some worldview or another, there is not likely to be a person who can encompass the differences among the worldviews.

What some have called this postmodern context is thus seemingly paradoxical with respect to creating leadership. We need to work together but we also need to hold fast to our differing worldviews. This would seem to make any possible direction in shared work equivocal, and yet is not leadership supposed to be about creating unity of purpose? Commitment in such contexts cannot be to some leader, or to people who do not share your values or your sense of truth. Thus commitment would seem to be limited to no more than a "process of engagement." Adaptive challenges, which are difficult in the best circumstances to articulate and understand, cannot be expressed in terms that differing perspectives can agree on. The taken-for-granted truths of the second principle—that leadership is a social influence process, that the leader is the person who has the most influence, that the leader can embrace differing perspectives and unify them—lose their power to make leadership happen in such contexts. As was the case with the limits of personal dominance and the emergence of interpersonal influence, some new principle of leadership is being called forth by these paradoxes.

Table 4.1 summarizes the capacities and limits of the second principle with respect to the leadership tasks.

**Table 4.1  Capacities and Limits of the Interpersonal Influence Principle with Respect to the Leadership Tasks**

| Tasks | Capacities of Interpersonal Influence | Limits of Interpersonal Influence |
|---|---|---|
| Setting direction | The leader is understood to create a shared vision by encompassing and integrating a variety of differing perspectives. | When direction becomes equivocal as a result of sharing work across differing worldviews, the capacity of a leader to negotiate some unifying vision is greatly reduced. |
| Creating commitment | Commitment is created to the shared vision held and articulated by the leader. | When the leader's vision can no longer hold and articulate multiple worldviews, commitment is reduced. |
| Facing adaptive challenge | More challenges can be recognized and addressed because multiple perspectives are enabled; the climate for innovation can improve. | Challenges arising in contexts of equivocal difference fail to be recognized as tasks approachable by leadership. |

*An engineer from Musitron sat with Raul after the first meeting of*
*the X Project Team, the designation of the cross-functional group*
*that was charged with developing the new digital-analog product. The*
*X stood for both the unknown nature of the new product and the fact*
*that it was being created across divisional lines. The engineer was*
*obviously more than a little frustrated.*

"This is not going to work, Raul," she said. "It's just out of
hand. I thought this was supposed to be a self-managed team."

"I know. It's natural for there to be some tough sledding at first."

"Someone needs to make sure the Zoffner people understand
what a self-managed team is, then, because they definitely saw themselves being in charge of the meeting."

"No. Come on, Lois. You know how they are, but they weren't
in charge."

"How about this? They had the meeting agenda on a flip chart
when we walked in the door. One of them led the meeting, just to
keep order, he said, but I know better. Whenever one of us would
bring up a topic, he would say they would add it to the agenda for discussion later. We never got to any of our topics. They were controlling the agenda."

"Listen to you, Lois. We, they, them, us. You've got to go through
the process of forming into a team. Give it some time."

"We're the division with the breakthrough technology, Raul.
Sure, they also have a lot to offer, but they're treating us like a supplier, not a full partner."

*Almost at the same time, a craftsman was walking the shop floor*
*with Eddie over at Zoffner.*

"It was like they were deliberately trying to break up the meeting. If they don't want to do this, why should we?"

*"I don't care whether they want to do this or not. I'll get some-
one else if you can't handle it. This project is going to happen and it's
going to work, damn it, and it's your job to make sure it works!"*

*"OK, OK, Eddie. I understand. It's just frustrating, you know?
We don't know what it is we're developing. We looked at some
plans they brought with them, but to tell you the truth, I wasn't getting it. Too much jargon. I could tell they were thinking we were
pretty stupid."*

*"Sure, but those plans are just a starting place anyway. Forget
that. Focus on the future. On what you're going to develop. Don't
let jargon get in your way of influencing the direction of the project.
They'll be pushing their agenda, make sure you're pushing ours."*

*"I did that. But get this. I brought up that the final product would
have to meet Zoffner quality standards and they said, right, or Musitron standards. Has it been decided what brand this thing will have?
Because they must think it will be a Musitron product."*

*"It hasn't been decided. It won't be decided until there's a prod-
uct to decide about. But it's going to be a real piano, at least part of
it is, and so it's going to have to come up to our standards. Just bide
your time on that. Let's just see how things develop."*

## Connecting the Story to the Limits

Naturally the two sides of this cross-functional team are unfamiliar
with one another and therefore somewhat suspicious. Naturally
they don't speak the same language and they make different assumptions. They face the classic developmental tasks (forming,
storming, norming, performing) to become a functioning team.
Given that they acknowledge shared work, they will in time get
themselves into some kind of shape. The question most pressing

here is one of accomplishing the leadership tasks. How would such a team create leadership for itself?

We might suppose that this is not a matter for the members to do for themselves, but a matter for Elena, Raul, and Eddie to take care of. Leadership in this case can be seen as a top-management responsibility, and the top leaders should be making sure that the team has a clear direction, that its members get committed, and that when the team runs into challenges, the top management should provide guidance.

The limitation of this approach is that top managers may be in no better position to accomplish these leadership tasks than the team members are. Leaving the leadership tasks to be performed by top management adds another worldview into the mix, and one that, in a case such as this, is in no better position to provide the resolving embrace and integration of the differing cultures than are the members of the team.

In spite of these limitations, many, if not most, organizations facing this kind of challenge will depend on higher levels of management to provide leadership, while declaring that the project team is self-managed. Justifiably, people in the organization will say that this is hypocritical. Perhaps, however, it is more the result of confusion and ambiguity, the kind of uncertainty that attends the loss of the second principle's capacity to make sense of leadership.

Some organizations will try to go toward the discomfort and ambiguity, exploring the growing edges of some as yet unknown sense of how direction can be set, commitment created, and adaptive challenges faced while holding two worldviews each equally worthy of its own integrity. This is courageous, but—lacking some more adequate way of understanding leadership—likely to reach its own kind of impasse. For the courageous organization is likely to discover that holding two worldviews without an embracing integration will lead to direction that is equivocal and commitment that is weak or nonexistent outside of the perspectival (in this case, divisional) boundaries. Such a situation will engender an adaptive challenge without providing any capacity to articulate it, much less face it.

Let's fast-forward a couple of months in our story, and then take a closer look at how encountering the limits of the second principle can play out in an organization.

*Raul was the first to suggest that the cross-functional team needed some support in the face of the challenges that were being thrown at it. The leadership council agreed and an experienced facilitator and team-development specialist was hired to work with the team. The group went off for the better part of a week for team building, which did in fact bring the members closer together and helped greatly in getting everyone to see that they were one team with a single task and that they would need to come together if their shared work was to get done. "We need to be us, not we and they," was how one of them put it at the end of the week.*

*The facilitator then began to sit in on their team meetings while they were doing their work. She gently but insistently used timely feedback to show them the importance of respecting one another and their differing points of view. She helped them gradually learn how to pay attention to their process as well as their product, to not allow one or two people to dominate the discussions, and to balance advocacy and inquiry. They worked hard to put into practice what she was showing them. Soon it began to have an effect. The X Team began to work with more progress on the design of the new product.*

*As they did this, there were certain subjects that they learned were a little too hot to handle: the name of the new product and its brand designation, where and how it would be manufactured and to what standards, even what its market was intended to be. These subjects were too hot because they tended to take the team away from its sense of unity back toward its two underlying perspectival home bases, Zoffner Piano and Musitron. Most of the time and for most topics, the importance of these worldviews could be suppressed in favor of getting on with the job. At the first quarterly report by the team to the leadership council, something of the labor involved in trying to create a unity embracing diversity could be detected. The presentation was in two parts, one presented by an engineer from Musitron, the second by a craftsman from Zoffner Piano.*

*"After some initial difficulty," the Musitron engineer reported, "the X Project is off to a good start." He offered a summary of what the team had accomplished so far and an overview of the three alternative designs the team was in the process of analyzing. As he was wrapping up, he said, "The X Product will thus combine the best of an analog instrument, with its sensitivity to nuances in the player's touch, with the best of digital technology. This will be a unique instrument, drawing on the beauty of real strings as the input to a digital system."*

*The team member from Zoffner Piano spoke next, covering what the team saw as its next steps and timelines for completion of each phase of work. Like his counterpart from Musitron, he rounded off his presentation with a little summary flourish at the end.*

*"The team feels confident that we will produce a unique and exciting piano. One that, as my colleague has already pointed out, has all of the features and quality a musician would expect in a Zoffner instrument along with the addition of exciting enhancements via digital technology."*

*The leadership council was pleased, of course, by this report of progress and also by the obvious enthusiasm of the team members. They were most pleased (and a little surprised) by the shared vision*

*for the final product that the team presented. There was a general*
*sense of relief and celebration after this meeting, and many of the X*
*Team members shook hands with one another and smiled proudly.*

*How hard it was for them, then, only a few months later, to dis-*
*cover that what they had thought was a clear and unified vision, a*
*shared sense of their shared work, turned out to be nothing more than*
*a temporarily useful misunderstanding.*

## How Unity Can Mask Diversity

Unity embracing diversity is not so easily achieved as this, even
given all the hard work the team put in. Let's explore more closely
what I am claiming is the likely outcome of holding two (or more)
worldviews as if each is equally worthy of its own integrity, while
continuing to take for granted the truths organized by the second
principle. Note that in the view I am offering, this is a context in
which a whole community is implicated and participates. There is
no useful way to understand this situation as something that an
individual leader has created or failed to avoid. It is the whole community that holds the worldviews as equals, and it is in the interactions of the whole community that leadership is understood to
happen according to the truths of interpersonal influence.

I claimed earlier that one likely outcome would be equivocal-
ity of direction. Yet this X Team seems to have achieved a common
sense of direction, clear and relatively unambiguous, allowing for
its place in the project cycle. But has it? If we listen carefully not
just to the content of each report but to the way the report is
framed (represented here by each summary statement), we may
begin to see through the unity and the shared vision (which is real
enough but not sufficient) and glimpse the original perspectival
home bases.

"This will be a unique instrument, drawing on the beauty of
real strings as the input to a digital system," says the engineer from
Musitron. Although this statement pays admirable tribute to the

worthiness of the traditional piano, it frames the new product in terms of a "digital system." The Musitron engineer frames the project as creating a digital instrument that uses real strings as an input device. In short (and somewhat unfairly oversimplifying the very real degree of common vision the team has achieved), the Musitron people are likely to see the new product as a Musitron product with a Zoffner enhancement.

The Zoffner craftsman winds up saying that the new instrument will have "all of the features and quality a musician would expect in a Zoffner instrument, with the addition of exciting enhancements via digital technology." Not surprisingly, the Zoffner people frame the new product as a piano with digital options.

These two frames for understanding the new product, when taken together, are equivocal with respect to direction. Each way of framing the work potentially results in a different final product. Someone might say this is not the case because the two frames are simply different ways to view the same thing, and so it really doesn't matter because only one product will come out in the end. The problem with this is that there is no "same thing" to view in two different ways. All they have to work with are the two different frameworks. There is not some product out there that is independent of these ways of thinking about it. A new product might be created that somehow satisfies both ways of framing it, but such a product might not make the best use of either technology, or such a product might not be possible at all.

Given these two differing ways of framing the work, the leadership task of setting direction is being accomplished in each of the perspectival communities that make up the cross-functional team. Direction makes sense from one framework or the other, but there is no framework from which the work of the X Project Team as a whole makes sense. Interpersonal influence is working away, creating leadership as effectively as ever within each of the perspectives. The capacity of interpersonal influence to make sense across the boundaries of these perspectives is limited, however, perhaps to the point that leadership on the level of the whole team does not exist.

The context is similar where creating commitment is concerned. What the team members take as commitment to the X Project Team may be more like an extension of their existing commitment to their own perspective: they are committed to the X Project Team as a field in which their home-base perspective can be recognized and honored. So long as the team can stay within some rules of conduct that specify how differing perspectives are to be appreciated and respected, this kind of secondhand commitment may work to bind the team as a whole. But when resources become scarce, or when decisions are being made that will necessarily force a choice between the values of one or the other perspective, the underlying lack of commitment to the shared work may surface. If that happens, turf battles will spring up, accusations that the other side was never really interested in working collaboratively will come from each side, and the prospects for bringing the project to an effective outcome will be greatly reduced.

This kind of thing is usually attributed to natural human competitiveness and territorial protectiveness. People can work together across the boundaries that divide them, some will say, until something is really at stake; then real human nature will show up. People can appreciate differing points of view and engage in dialogue so long as no one has any real skin in the game. But when push comes to shove, it's a dog-eat-dog world.

There is enough truth in this interpretation to make it believable, but from the perspective being offered here, it is more useful to understand what is happening in these contexts as a lack of leadership capacity to create commitment across certain kinds of boundaries. The problem is thus seen to be less about the inherently selfish and competitive nature of the human being, and more about the built-in limitations of a way of understanding leadership. The interpersonal influence principle does not provide effective tools for creating commitment across certain kinds of boundaries because influence is not likely to flow across boundaries that separate ways of making sense of the world. People with significantly differing values are unlikely to have much influence with one another. Leadership as constituted by the second principle reaches its limit when influence can no longer be negotiated interpersonally.

This much seems obvious. Yet it is one of those obvious things that is easily overlooked, especially in large, multifunctional organizations. We hear a lot of talk about creating a shared vision that will energize and inspire a whole complex organization. Yet if we entertain the notion that people within such an organization are more likely to be using the truths of the second principle to set direction, create commitment, and face challenges locally, within the boundaries of what makes sense locally, then leadership is likely to be much more powerfully effective within manufacturing, within finance, within sales, within human resources, and, yes, within the senior-management team, than it is across any of these perspectival boundaries. The prospects for a unifying vision would seem to come down to this: to the extent that the vision specifies a clear, relatively unequivocal direction, it will make sense to people in proportion to how close a given person's home-base perspective is to the perspective underlying the vision. To the extent that the vision will make sense to people throughout the organization, crossing boundaries of perspective and values, the vision will be abstract and equivocal.

In the old Zoffner Piano Company under Mr. Karl, his vision of making pianos that the average person could afford to buy for a son or daughter was specific and relatively unequivocal. Because the original company was virtually one community making sense of the world in one way, this vision was compelling for the whole organization. Now that Zoffner Music has two distinct and autonomous divisions with significantly differing ways of making sense of the world, an unequivocal vision is elusive. Elena cannot create such a vision, not because she lacks the leadership ability of her father but because the leadership principle she (along with the rest of the organization) is using to make leadership happen is limited in its capacity to create such a vision.

There is one way out of this. She could renounce the autonomy of the two divisions and insist that her perspective become integrative, the controlling point of view to which each division would become relativized. In effect, this would be to assert her prerogative as CEO to frame the principle by which the organization would make leadership happen. (Note that people in the organization may or may not recognize that leadership is happening as a result.) I suspect that this solution is employed quite often in organizations, but I also suspect that its effectiveness tends to be limited. Where and when it has become important to recognize the integrity and wholeness of differing perspectives, such subordination of perspectives to a controlling point of view will encounter definite limitations.

This is not to say that an abstract and equivocal vision will not in some sense create unity in a complex organization. But the unity it creates will be a unity subordinating and masking diversity, and this is not the same as a unity coordinating and embracing diversity. The prospect for this kind of unity depends on the emergence of a third leadership principle that will overcome the limitations of interpersonal influence.

*It happened one day about six months into the X Project. The occasion was a presentation by an industrial design firm the team had hired to create a physical design for the new instrument. For weeks a subteam had been working with the design firm people to help them understand the nature of the new product. Because the Musitron people had the most experience at working with industrial designers, this subteam was composed exclusively of Musitron people. No one had any reason to give this arrangement any thought. The team was convinced of its basic agreement on the nature and capabilities of the new instrument. After all, it was all captured in a lengthy and detailed report to the leadership council, and the council had approved the move to begin production.*

*So when the industrial designer revealed the result of his work, jaws dropped all around the table. Later the people from Zoffner*

Piano said it felt like they had been hit in the stomach. The Musitron people were perplexed and some even felt angered by what they saw as a betrayal of the project team by the piano division.

"This is what we agreed on, Raul," the engineer from Musitron said to his boss later. "I think it just never occurred to them to think what such a thing would actually turn out to be. They were blinded by their need for it to be a regular piano, I guess."

What the designer had revealed was anything but a regular piano. Through the eyes of the piano division people it looked like a monstrosity. It was sleek and rounded and looked more like a huge designer computer than a piano. It had a row of buttons above the keyboard and a computer screen behind the music holder and speaker vents cut into each side of the front. Its surface was hard looking and had a suspicious sheen. The case was to be made of a carbon-fiber composite material.

"But you must have wood for the sound!" someone from the piano division gasped.

"No, the electronics will produce the final sound. It doesn't matter what material the case is made of. The carbon-fiber will be lighter, less costly, easier to manufacture, and more durable."

"But it won't be a piano! We were making a piano. Did you forget that?"

"What do you mean? We were making a new product, like nothing ever seen before. Surely you didn't expect it to be an ordinary spinet."

Elena wanted to know just one thing: How could this happen? How could the team members work together for all that time without realizing that they basically disagreed about what they were working on?

*"It literally never came up," Raul explained. "I've talked to almost everyone on the team, and they are embarrassed by it because it seems so obvious in hindsight, but they actually never had a conversation about the instrument's physical specifications. They focused on its features, what it would do, how people would use it. The piano people were assuming all along that everything being talked about would somehow be incorporated into a piano. They didn't have the experience with the electronics to know what modifications would have to be made, but they assumed that they would be made starting with a traditional piano. The Musitron people thought it was too obvious to state that the kind of features they were talking about couldn't be incorporated into anything like a traditional piano. So when they would talk about the instrument having speakers, for example, the Musitron people were seeing speaker vents on the front, while the Zoffner people were imagining speakers hidden away somehow. Same for all the features. Whatever they talked about, each group assimilated to their preexisting notions of the final product."*

*"They were working on two different products the whole time," Elena said, shaking her head. "So where are we now?"*

*"I don't know. It looks bad. The Musitron people want to go ahead, of course, but the piano people are saying that there is no way they can manufacture the instrument. They see it as a Musitron project now. The whole idea of doing something across the divisions seems to be breaking down."*

## Conclusion

Though this may be something of an exaggeration to make a point, I wonder how often cross-functional teams or other groups trying to work across some significant boundary end up with a version of this outcome. The boundary need not be as dramatic as that between Zoffner Piano and Musitron. It could even happen within a single function, and in some ways may be even more likely when the boundary is more subtle. Within a single marketing function, for example, two camps may form around differing marketing approaches or philosophies and the seeming unity of the function may mask the subtle but significant differences in how people understand what they are doing.

At the same time, there will be powerful reasons for people in this marketing function to understand themselves as a single, unified entity. They are organized as a single unit within the larger organization; they all report to the same boss; they may be located together and have daily contact; and, most important, they share work—often across the subtle boundary within. The context of unity, the reasons for remaining unified and thinking of themselves as one unit, will likely result in their diversity being masked. Their differences will become a topic that cannot be discussed for fear of dividing what must be united.

In addition to the effects this may have on the group's performance of its marketing work, it also decreases the capacity to make sense of leadership and to accomplish the leadership tasks. If leadership in such a function is being understood from the perspective of the second principle, and if the person understood to be the leader is an adherent of one or the other of the two camps and is unable to encompass and integrate the two points of view, direction will likely be equivocal and commitment will be more to one of the differing philosophies and less to the function as a whole. The response of such a secretly bifurcated group to an adaptive challenge, one that significantly calls into question one or both of the differing approaches and creates uncertainty and pressure to act without clear understanding, may be to fall apart into the two camps because direction and commitment are stronger there than within the masking unity. In a situation in which meaning is threatened, people will align with whatever can provide the most meaning.

This is the situation, admittedly dramatized, at Zoffner Music. The emerging context in which the business is being called to operate is an order of magnitude more complex than the leadership principle its people are using has the capacity to handle. They can't make sense of the leadership tasks, not because they lack good leaders but because the second principle, interpersonal influence, is inadequate to the context.

I hope by now I have been able to make it clear that this is not a situational phenomenon that can be addressed by a change in leadership style. I am not suggesting that what needs to happen is that Elena (or anyone) needs to adopt a more (or a less) participative approach, or focus more on relationships, or become more or less directive, or change in any way what we might call leadership behavior. Nothing less than a revolution of mind is required, a shift in order of thought, a reformation of how leadership is known.

This is the challenge being faced by many communities and organizations as the world becomes more connected and interdependent. The very idea of leadership—what it is and how it works and how people even know it when they see it—is in the process of changing. Just what the idea of leadership might be about to become is the topic of the next chapter.

*Chapter Five*

# Relational Dialogue

Truth, far from being a solemn and severe master, is
a docile and obedient servant.
—*Nelson Goodman*, Ways of Worldmaking

Here is the challenging context that I believe is giving rise to a third
leadership principle: When there is shared work among people who
make sense of that work and the world from differing worldviews,
how can those people accomplish the leadership tasks while holding their differing worldviews as equally worthy and warrantable?

The first principle, personal dominance, assimilates differing
worldviews (if they exist) to the worldview of the leader. The leader
and the followers bend and blend whatever differences in worldview they have in order to create the capacity to accomplish the
leadership tasks. (They trade off whatever benefit might derive
from maintaining differences to attain the benefit of clear, univocal
leadership.) The wider the differences in worldview, the less likely
that personal dominance can assimilate differing views, which
leads to limits on the capacity of the first principle to make sense of
leadership in contexts of significant difference.

The second principle, interpersonal influence, increases the
range of differences that can be included in the leadership process
by allowing a negotiation of influence that results in the identification of a person whose view is wide enough or flexible enough
to accommodate differing views. Accommodation allows for differing views to be contained with some degree of integrity within
the leader's view. The leader and followers integrate differences

and relativize views to a larger view held by the leader. Differences are retained but they are ordered in relation to an encompassing view. The second principle can accomplish the leadership tasks while taking in widely differing views so long as one view can be constructed that encompasses the others.

What are we to make of contexts in which worldviews are to be held as equally important, equally valid, equally warrantable, and exactly what is *not* wanted is the assimilation or the accommodation of some views to a controlling or encompassing view? Then how will the leadership tasks get accomplished? To answer this question and confront this challenge of our own making, some new leadership principle is being called forth, one that will organize truths capable of making sense of leadership in a context of enduring difference, of unity embracing diversity. How might such a principle emerge?

## Demands of a New Form of Living

Leadership principles come into being when there's no other way. Personal dominance and interpersonal influence will continue to afford useful ways of understanding leadership in many, if not most, contexts of human activity, and no third principle would be required if these contexts were the only ones in need of leadership. But this does not appear to be the case. By inventing ways to interconnect the whole planet, we humans seem to have brought about a new form of living. We don't yet know what to call this new form of living, but we know it is coming after some other forms of living we do have names for; and so we tend to call it things like *post-industrial* and *postmodern*.

The interconnection of the world is not just global. It's also local. Just as different parts of the world are interconnected, so are different parts of our communities, and different parts of organizations, and different groups of people. The interconnection is pervasive, from the instant messages my daughter exchanges with her friends on the Internet to the interconnection of the global economy.

So what? How does this pervasive interconnection bring about a new form of living and create contexts in need of leadership for which neither dominance nor interpersonal influence are useful ways of making that leadership happen? To approach the answer (well, my answer) to this question, let's stop to consider some examples of things that are happening these days where I think a third leadership principle is being called forth because neither the first nor the second principle can make leadership happen.

### Examples of Contexts That Call Forth a Third Principle

City council members of opposite and clashing political beliefs serve together over a period of years and gradually come to some common understanding of what they can and cannot accomplish given their differences. Although holding tightly to differing political philosophies, values, and beliefs, they recognize that they have a duty as elected officials no matter what their differences. Calls are made from every side for the council to work together. Although this may be political posturing, even such political posturing plays a role in creating a common understanding. The very act of resisting and countering proposals from "the opposition" constitutes implicit acknowledgment of a shared duty. Actions taken by some individuals counter to this duty (for example, statements of the "poisoning the well" variety) tend to be criticized from all sides.

Key managers in a large telecommunications company wrestle across their functional boundaries to understand a rapidly changing competitive environment. Rooted in the traditional business of telephony, with billions of dollars invested in the physical infrastructure of lines and switches and confronted with the emergence of the Internet (where competitors have gotten far ahead of the game), these managers struggle together to understand how to move from the solid realities of the past toward the unknown potential of the future. There is no single perspective from which this challenge becomes intelligible. It can only hope to be understood and acted on from multiple perspectives.

The citizens of a community form a committee across economic, racial, and social lines with the intent of redrawing school districts in the hopes of improving the quality of education for their children. After a long period of struggle, they give up, seemingly overwhelmed by the differing values, perspectives, beliefs, truths, and convictions brought into the committee, all of which the committee at least in principle tried to honor.

American and Egyptian investigators announce that they are on a joint search for the truth of what happened to EgyptAir Flight 990. The words of the copilot, acknowledged as the same words by both camps of investigators, are interpreted according to differing cultural lenses. It is likely that any truth found or constructed in this search will have to be viewed from within one or the other of the two cultural worldviews. There will be truth, but not the same truth.

Irish Republicans and Unionists search in agony and bloodshed for a country they can live in together. If, as I suppose, the aim of the two sides changed at some point in the history of this conflict from that of mutual destruction to finding a way out of the conflict, what difference did this make? While each side holds fast to its belief in its own worldview, each side also begins to admit the possibility that the other side is also worthy of belief. Once this is admitted as possible, multiple realities are admitted and the whole context changes.

A corporation with operations in countries around the world seeks to create a global organization. The values, visions, plans, and strategies of such an organization will be interpreted and reinterpreted within many differing cultures. Can even a simple mission statement be univocal across languages and cultures? If not, how can a complex strategy be implemented as if it were a single, unified plan?

Faculty members in a high school ask themselves what they can take responsibility for in their school as a leadership team in light of existing power structures in the school system. How can the school principal, for example, be both the sole authority in the school (as recognized by the district office) and be a more or less equal member of the leadership team at the same time? Likewise, how can the teachers on the team understand themselves as having meaningful responsibility in the school while simultaneously knowing that the principal is ultimately responsible?

I want to suggest that each of these examples is more than an example of a context in need of leadership, each is also an example of *the attempt to bring forth a new principle of leadership*. I realize that some of these examples may not seem appropriate for the consideration of leadership at all. They may seem to be contexts of conflict, compromise, or just good old-fashioned messes. They may seem at best to describe not leadership but the lack of leadership. And so they do. And yet, as I am suggesting, this lack of leadership comes about not because of a lack of leaders who could provide leadership in these contexts (which would suggest that the solution is to develop more and better leaders), but because the principles of leadership we already have are not capable of making leadership happen in these contexts. Instead of needing more and better leaders, I believe that only a new principle of leadership can make leadership happen in contexts such as these—and that as we continue to create more and more contexts like these, such a new principle is being worked out. To develop leadership in our communities and organizations, then, we need to explore just what truths this new principle organizes and discover how we can support people in bringing a third principle forth and putting it to use.

### Common Elements of the Examples

It is useful as a first step in exploring this emerging third principle to look more closely at these examples. What, in short, are the aspects of these examples that represent a working out of a third leadership principle?

*Mutual Acknowledgment of Shared Work.* The first thing to notice about each example is a mutual acknowledgment of shared work. Although in each there are distinctly differing perspectives present, and in some of the examples these differences represent conflict and even animosity and violence, these differences do not prevent people from seeing that somehow they are in it together. There are many contexts that might appear to be similar to the examples given but lack this critical aspect. The tragedy in Kosovo, for example, looks like a context in which there is no acknowledgment of shared work. For as long as most of us can remember, the conflict in the Middle East has been especially devoid of any sense of shared work. Wars in general would seem to be contexts in which differing worldviews do not acknowledge shared work. In general when differing worldviews seek each other's destruction there is no shared work, for what each side seeks is mutually exclusive of what the other side seeks. (Such mutually destructive worldviews are, however, aspects of the identity of each. Part of what it means to be a person holding one worldview in such violent contexts is to have a person holding the other worldview as an enemy. Only when such enemies come to acknowledge shared work is leadership called forth.)

The increasingly vitriolic context of U.S. national (and much local) politics may also represent a context in which politicians have backed away from acknowledging shared work. The decreasing recognition of shared work across political boundaries may be why there is so much distress over negative campaigning, gridlock, and the general debasement of public discourse. It is not these things in themselves that are so distressing, but what is being lost—the sense that we are in the end all in this together, the sense of shared work.

The situation among Israel, its Arab neighbors, and the Palestinians at this writing is perhaps on the cusp of moving from a context of mutual destruction to one in which there is an acknowledgment of shared work. If the Palestinians have in fact revoked their pledge to destroy Israel, and if Israel does in fact recognize the right of Palestinians to a state, then the so-called final status negotiations will represent a mutual acknowledgment of shared work and some leadership principle will be called forth to accomplish the leadership tasks across these antagonistic differences.

Mutually acknowledging shared work calls forth leadership. But notice what the mutual acknowledgment of shared work does not mean. It does not mean agreement. It does not mean that conflict, including violent conflict, is over. It does not mean there is a shared understanding of the work, a shared valuing of all possible outcomes, or shared understanding of any challenge or problem creating the work. In other words, mutual acknowledgment of shared work does not in itself solve the underlying problems or conflicts. It does, however, create the possibility of leadership. It frames the context in a way that opens up the possibility that there are leadership tasks waiting to be accomplished, and thus leadership is being called forth.

***Differing Worldviews Are Held as Equally Worthy.*** The second thing to notice about these examples is that although each is characterized by the presence of differing worldviews, no worldview is usefully understood as the controlling or encompassing view to which the others are relativized. I say "usefully understood," because although people in such contexts may still understand their own worldview as being more natural or more real than any other, this understanding tends to decrease the capacity for leadership. What is called forth in these contexts is a kind of equal gravity for each worldview. Each asserts its own integrity, the meaningfulness and importance of its own terms, the logic of its own system. To the extent that these assertions are honored, the prospects for relational dialogue increase.

This is true whether the worldviews in question encompass large cultural, ethnic, and historical differences or smaller, more ephemeral local differences. Thus the difference in worldviews between cultures has similar effect in these contexts as the difference in worldviews between organizational functions or professions. What matters is not how hard it may be to work across the boundary of the difference, the depth of the gulf, but that the worldviews on either side move toward mutual regard.

This is noticeable in any organization that resolves to be more customer oriented. As the conventional wisdom would rightly have it, customers do not care about the (internally important) differences among separate functions and operational divisions of the organization. Customers are disinterested with respect to the relative importance and regard of an organization's various functions. To become customer focused often means ignoring traditional ways of ordering and relativizing internal divisions. Traditional (and meaningful) functional emphases must be replaced by new, untested patterns of organization and interaction more responsive to external needs. The effects within the organization can be far-reaching, affecting everything from the compensation system to the way work flows to the overall culture of the organization. And especially the way leadership happens. The traditional dependence on hierarchical authority (which strongly supports both personal dominance and interpersonal influence) often results in a decrease in leadership, less sense of direction, lower commitment, and a smaller capacity to confront adaptive challenges. The question "Who's in charge here?" finds no ready answer. The search is on for some new way to accomplish the leadership tasks.

In short, when no one perspective is adequate for creating understanding or action, for accomplishing the leadership tasks, multiple perspectives come into play. The question then becomes, How can leadership happen using multiple (and sometimes conflicted) worldviews?

**The Leadership Tasks, Though Relevant and Pressing, Cannot Be Accomplished.** The third thing to notice about these examples is that there is some need to accomplish the leadership tasks growing out of the mutual acknowledgment of shared work. Once people see that there is work between them, the leadership tasks become relevant: how to set direction, create commitment, face adaptive challenges.

The problem is that seeing shared work, while it makes the leadership tasks relevant, does not resolve the differences or engender unity and thus does not in itself afford an approach to accomplishing the leadership tasks. The tasks are there, and they are pressing, but accomplishing them is not yet possible, because there is no cross-worldview agreement about what that direction would look like, what there is to commit to, or how an adaptive challenge would even be framed.

Of course, from within each worldview, leadership can still be happening. Within each worldview, the accomplishment of the leadership tasks is quite possible. Unfortunately, this increases the problem. Making sense of direction from a marketing perspective provides meaning to people in marketing, but this very sense of meaning can be a block to making sense across the boundary between, say, marketing and R&D. "Why can't they see that we already have the answer?"

***No Leader Can Create Leadership.***  In each example, no person is recognized as the leader across the worldviews if by leader it is understood that such a person will create leadership, either directly and personally as with the first principle, or indirectly and interpersonally by holding an encompassing perspective as with the second principle. For example, although the CEO of the telecommunications company may seem to be able to provide leadership by virtue of having an overview of the differing perspectives comprising the traditional world of telephony and the emerging world of the Internet, such an overview, even if it is possible, does not enable the CEO to gain a measure of influence greater than the influences existing within the perspectives. Instead, the CEO's overview abstracts elements of each perspective, viewing each from a high level, leaving out the world of details that make up the perspectives themselves. (In other words, it's difficult if not impossible to gain influence within a worldview if you only see that world from 50,000 feet.) These are thus contexts in which no leader has the capacity to create leadership (except within the worldviews), which is why they strike us as situations crying out for leadership or as conflicts that are naturally immune to leadership.

It might seem paradoxical that in each of these examples, the emergence of a leader (as understood from the perspective of the first or second principle) would seem to decrease the chances that leadership could happen across worldviews. The emergence of a dominant or influencing leader would likely result in the promotion of one worldview into a place of honor and the subordination of other perspectives. The equal gravity of the differing perspectives would be given up in order to make leadership happen by making sense from a single unifying perspective (as with the second principle). Although this might be useful in some instances, I submit that the increasing interconnectedness of worldviews is calling this way of creating leadership into question and that an approach to making leadership happen that does not trade off the equal worthiness of differing worldviews is being sought.

### *Summary of Features Calling Forth a Third Principle*

For quick reference, here are the features of life that I hypothesize are in the process of being transformed into a third leadership principle:

- People holding differing worldviews are involved in mutually acknowledged shared work.
- The differing worldviews are held as if they were equally worthy, true, real.
- The leadership tasks are relevant but not capable of being accomplished across worldviews.
- No person can be the leader and create leadership without giving up the equal gravity of the differing perspectives.

## Proposed Truths of a Third Principle

As I have said, leadership principles organize some taken-for-granted truths so that people recognize leadership when it happens and the leadership tasks can thus be accomplished. Such principles, remember, are proposed as achievements of a community, of people thinking, talking, and working together.

In thinking about an emerging third principle we come up against a problem. In some ways it is the opposite problem we have had so far. So far, I have focused on exploring the truth of some taken-for-granted truths. In other words, I have taken ideas that are usually accepted as naturally and obviously true (some people are dominant, some people have more influence than others) and have tried to reframe them as useful agreements among people who need to so agree in order to recognize leadership. While not asserting that they are not true, I have not exactly reaffirmed them as certainly true. My position has been more that they are provisionally and usefully true, which is all that matters practically.

Now we come to the need to articulate some taken-for-granted truths that might be organized by a third leadership principle I call *relational dialogue*, and the shoe is on the other foot. What I will now present will more than likely strike you as being radically open to question, not taken for granted at all. The ideas (I better not call them truths just yet) articulated here are I believe in the process of becoming truths (or being recognized as true). It is the working out, the creation, or the discovery of just how they are true that constitutes the emergence of the third leadership principle. In other words, so long as these ideas (or any other ideas proposed in their place) are merely ideas and are not taken for granted as truths, they cannot be put to use to make leadership happen simply because, without being taken as true, they cannot pervasively make sense in a community. They will be interesting ideas about leadership but will lack the capacity to make leadership happen.

So what are these ideas that I claim are truths-in-the-making for use as a third leadership principle? There are, I propose, four that are especially important. Here is the first.

## People Make Sense of Reality Through Relational Processes

The philosophical question of whether reality is found or constructed (which is by its nature only discussible, not finally answerable) is less important here than the practical question of how people who understand the world in differing ways can talk together, think together, and work together. I want to suggest that for strictly practical reasons this idea is moving toward being an accepted fact: that people construct reality through their interactions within worldviews.

It is highly practical and useful for the development of a third leadership principle to understand that people construct *a* (not *the*) reality when they explain things to one another, tell each other stories, create models and theories (such as this one), and write about all this in books; when they offer intuitions to others for consideration, form judgments and test them with others in word and action, and evaluate outcomes and work with others to improve outcomes according to set criteria; and generally when they interact through thought, word, and action to bring into being what is important, worthy, real, and actual. In other words, people live from day to day in continuous interaction with and knowledge of others, and it is a day-to-day practical reality that is so usefully understood as a relational construction.

Consider the extent to which I myself live from day to day within the embrace of a relational construction—the interactions I have and repeat countless times with my wife and daughters, and with friends, co-workers, bagel store clerks, newspaper columnists, lunchtime card players, fellow airline passengers, strangers. Living in this way, how do I know the answers to questions such as who am I, what are my values, what makes me angry or happy, what do I hope for, what are my dreams? The first reaction is that I know these things about myself because, well, they are a part of me, inside my head and I came over time to finally know myself. True enough. Yet at the same time, nothing I know about myself came out of nowhere; it all came from somewhere, and the relational truth that I am claiming is coming into being here points to how all the things I know about myself started outside me and worked their way in.

To answer the question of who I am, I am forced to use words, ideas, thoughts, and feelings that I get from only one place: the world of the people with whom I interrelate and interact. I literally cannot think of myself without participating in a shared vocabulary of concepts, ideas, feelings, values, and truths that I know because I am relationally connected to other people. Likewise the values that I hold dear come into being through my participation in a grand conversation about what is right and what is important that was going on before I was born and will continue after I am gone.

But what about things that make me angry or happy? Surely these are purely personal. Not if *purely personal* means separated from the relational context. Anger may be a physiological reaction and is thus perhaps purely personal biologically, but what makes that physiological reaction happen? Does it make me angry to see someone yawn? No. There are people who participate in relational processes different from mine who do experience the strictly biological reaction of anger upon seeing someone yawn. Does it make me happy to see it rain? No? Yes? The answer depends, does it not, on what relational communities and processes I participate in, on how the occurrence of rain is taken among the people with whom I interrelate and interact on a day-to-day basis. Ah, you say, but don't you get a secret pleasure in hearing the rain falling on the roof, in the cozy feeling of being warm and dry while it is wet and cold outside? But if this is my secret pleasure, how can you know about it and describe it? Exactly how is it a secret?

What about my most private aspirations, my hopes and dreams? Surely there are things about which I have never spoken to anyone and about which no one has ever spoken to me; strictly personal and often only half-formed wonderings about what I might do or become. What of these? Granted, I have thoughts that no other person has access to, but a lack of access does not imply a lack of connection in the creation. I might have no access to your money in the bank, but I participate in the creation of wealth through my labor, earning, and spending. Likewise others may have no access to my thoughts, but they participate in the creation of what can be thought, what can be hoped for, even what can be faintly glimpsed. The most original and creative ideas, works of art, books, poems, and scientific theories are each created by an individual who must, who cannot avoid, participating in some community, some culture, some net of relations in which the most original idea is warranted, made sense of, granted meaning.

All of what we take as reality (the reality that we move through and live in day to day, if not the larger reality of the universe) is something we construct in participation with others. We are who we are not by virtue of simply being someone, but by virtue of being someone in relation to others. Take for example the fact of being a parent. We usually think of this as someone we simply are. (This usual way of thinking is another aspect of our participation in certain kinds of relationships embedded in an individualistic culture.) But of course, there is another way to see being a parent, equally worthy and I think more useful: we are parents by virtue of our relationship with a child and with a world of parenting. It is not mere biological procreation that makes a parent but a whole form of living that sweeps us up in feedings, diapers, camp, T-ball, school projects, first dates, graduations, leaving home, and worry, worry, worry as only a parent can worry. To *be* a parent is to *participate* in a world that is constructed along with other people being parents (and friends and teachers and bankers and strangers).

Have I digressed too far from the topic of leadership? Why all this philosophy about the nature of being and reality? Just because this is a truth in the making. Explanation, exemplification, argument, and (sound or specious, depending on you point of view) reasoning about ideas among people is the process of an idea that is beginning to be taken for granted. It is precisely my hypothesis that this idea (or some alternative articulation of it) will become taken for granted and that as a taken-for-granted idea it will be one of the key elements organized into a principle by which people will create leadership, make leadership happen across boundaries of equal difference.

### Leadership Across Worldviews
### Requires Relational Dialogue

The first idea will need to become taken for granted as true because leadership can only be recognized as possible across worldviews to the extent that people take it for granted that reality is made sense of relationally and not simply found or discovered. This is the second truth-in-the-making.

The idea that what is real is simply waiting to be found supports and actively promotes the assertion that this worldview, these values, these beliefs actually conform to that ultimate reality, whereas that worldview, those values, and those beliefs unfortunately do not and so are not so valuable or believable as those people think. This in turn diminishes if not eliminates the opportunity for differing worldviews to be held as equally worthy, true, real.

What is the big difference between a reality that is found and one that is made sense of relationally? As suggested in the preceding section, the difference that makes the big difference has to do with how we think about individuals. If what is real can be found, then anyone can find it. An individual person can go out there and say, in effect, "What have we here? What a nice chunk of reality I have here. Let's go tell everyone about what I've found." And this person, understanding that he or she has found what is real, what is true, what is important, may then gain some power and influence as the individual possessor of a unique truth. In telling others about this found truth, this person becomes the authority on it, the interpreter of it, the giver of it, while others become the receivers. This is just how the doctrine that reality can be found supports the first and second leadership principles.

So long as we hold to the doctrine of found reality, we will be likely to hold to the idea that leadership is possessed by leaders, by people who have some special access to a found reality (their vision, creativity, passion) the possession of which can make them leaders. And so long as we hold to the truth that leaders possess leadership we will likely hold to the truth that leaders create leadership. Holding to this truth, in turn, may actually decrease the opportunity to make leadership happen across worldviews, because of the likely possibility that leadership created by a leader will work only within some specific worldview and not across worldviews.

Of course, this is an overstatement to make a point. Not all differing worldviews are so hard to encompass, and people of remarkable sensitivity and intelligence do encompass differing perspectives and so create leadership that embraces difference. I wonder, however, whether leaders who can make leadership work across such boundaries do in fact loosen their hold on the truth of their own ideas to the extent to which they succeed in crossing the boundaries.

In many of the contexts arising in the world today, however, there is no way to understand that a person could accomplish the leadership tasks while speaking the language, as it were, of a home-base perspective. The shared understanding across worldviews required to set direction, create commitment, and face adaptive challenges across worldviews would be missing. Only if a person could somehow move into the *space between worldviews* would an individual gain the capacity to speak across those worldviews. The leadership tasks must be accomplished somehow *between* the differing perspectives or versions of the world. But what (or where, or how) is this space in between worldviews? Is there indeed any space between worldviews to get into? How one answers this question is important for the way one approaches leadership in an increasingly interconnected world.

If one says yes, there is a ready-made world to find out there, and all the differing worldviews are alternative ways of knowing (of finding) that one natural world, then one tends to reach the conclusion that a leader could see that independent world better, more clearly, more completely than anyone else. Thus a person could get in between worldviews by finding the real world and thus seeing it more clearly than others. This might be called greater objectivity, or more penetrating vision, or deeper intuition. And objectivity, vision, and intuition could be understood as critical achievements of the leader that enable the creation of leadership, even across worldviews.

If, on the other hand, one says no, there is no ready-made world out there to find, there are only ways of making sense relationally, and whatever is actual and real is what is relationally constructed into one or another worldview, then one tends to reach the conclusion that a person could not see beyond worldviews to a world independent of worldviews, but could only see (or see with) some other worldview. Thus no person could see an independent world better, or more clearly, or more completely than anyone else. People can only see better, more clearly, more completely within some worldview. In other words, there is no space between worldviews to get into. Objectivity is objective only within some worldview (the objectivity of science, the objectivity of an art judge) and a vision only penetrates deeper into some worldview, and intuition divines truths previously undiscovered within a worldview. And thus objectivity, vision, and intuition can only enable a person to create leadership within some worldview, and there is no way to get between worldviews because worldviews take up all the mindspace there is.

Although I obviously take the second answer (there is no ready-made world to get to know better, only worldviews) as the truth, I appreciate the truth of the first answer. My argument here is that in a world that is increasingly in the process of interconnecting different worldviews, it is becoming increasingly difficult to maintain the first answer. For to do so in the end puts one in the position of saying that some view of the world and of life is more accurate, closer to a found world that is independent of ways of knowing, and therefore more true and more worthy of being preserved, honored, and acted on. It is an answer to a philosophical question that can result in some form of living, some worldview, being judged as naturally subordinate to a more complete and more compellingly real world-view. It is a philosophical position that supports understanding leadership in the form of the first and second principle, but decreases the possibility of understanding how leadership can happen in contexts of shared work across worldviews.

Where am I, having made these claims? Am I in the position of saying that anything goes? That reading tarot cards is as good a way to predict how molecules will react as scientific theory? Am I insisting that any and every worldview is somehow equal? That the truth is radically relative? The answer to some of these questions is a resounding no. The answer to others is probably yes.

No, anything doesn't go. Some worldviews destroy life, and these are unfit ways of knowing the world. They are not right in the sense that they do not work—they kill and propagate non-sense instead of making sense and meaning and promoting life—and they are not right in the sense that they seek the destruction of worldviews that do make sense and create meaning, that do promote life. There is no question that some worldviews are unfit for life and others are very fit indeed, but telling which is which is not always easy. So anything doesn't go, but it is not simply a matter of asserting the natural rightness of one's own perspective to tell what does go.

Reading tarot cards is (perhaps) a worldview, but I am not in any way claiming it has a capacity to make sense in some other worldview, which is what would be required for it to predict the behavior of molecules. In fact, I am asserting just the opposite—that it is very difficult, if not impossible, to make sense across worldviews. The possibility of encountering hardships as a result of turning up the knave of hearts (or whatever) makes sense of life only within the sense made relationally within the tarot world. It simply lacks the capacity to make sense outside that context.

So comparing worldviews is tricky, and saying that they are held as if they are equally worthy is not the same as saying that one worldview is as good for something as another worldview. World-views are equal in that they are equally capable of making sense of life for the people who relationally interact within a worldview. The sense made of life cannot be compared across worldviews. Each is good for what it is good for and nothing else. Some worldviews are good for a very great deal because they make sense of a great deal (religions, science, art, biography, politics), but this does not give credence to any claim that such a worldview is more real or more true than any other. It takes more as its subject of sensemaking, is more ambitious in constructing its truths, but cannot get outside of itself no matter how big it is.

Is the truth radically relative? Probably yes, but this does not make it any less valuable or any less true. Truths are constructed within worldviews. The truth of the tarot is limited to that worldview. Likewise, the truth of the ego and the id is limited to a depth psychology worldview (which you may participate in and thus come to believe in its truths), and the truth of simultaneous pair creation is limited to quantum physics. But just because you can't apply the truth of quantum physics to painting a landscape doesn't mean it is any less true. And just because you would not apply the truth of the tarot to your everyday life, that does not make it less true—within the worldview that supports it. In other words, we cannot have it both ways: claiming, for example, that the truths of science extend to every worldview while limiting tarot only to its narrow perspective.

Some truths are constructed in more than one worldview, such as the way both traditional psychology and, say, existential literature make sense of the individual in part with the truth that people are basically separate and ultimately alone. Although this makes such a truth more widely held, it does not mean that it is true because it conforms to a found world. Universal truths are constructed as universals within worldviews. Discovering that several worldviews construct similar truths does not mean that those severally constructed truths are somehow truer than any others and conform to some ultimate reality.

All this perhaps tedious discussion points to the conclusion that leadership can be recognized (and happen) across worldviews only to the extent that meaning, values, and thus direction, commitment, and adaptive responses can be constructed relationally (made sense of relationally) across worldviews. The leadership tasks can only be accomplished across worldviews if the people trying to accomplish them hold their own truths lightly, as it were, and appreciate the capacity of other worldviews to make up truths as well. The claim that this worldview is truer (conforms better to the "real" world) than that one limits us to the point of negating the possibility of creating leadership across worldviews.

But given all that I have claimed about the difficulty of doing this, is leadership not ruled out even when people understand that (and act as if) reality is relationally constructed? If there is no space between worldviews for people to get into, how can worldviews be bridged and connected? If people are somehow stuck within their ways of knowing, and if there are no larger truths for people to discover out there in a found world, how can differing worldviews ever be made to work together? This brings us to the next truth-in-the-making that will be needed to support the development of a third leadership principle.

### Leadership Happens When a Conversation Across Worldviews Makes Sense of a New Subject

Leadership across worldviews is recognized and thus happens when a conversation (an interaction, a conflict, a dialogue, an argument) that has been going on between or among worldviews creates, makes sense of, a new subject. This new subject might simply modify slightly the sense each worldview makes of the world, or it could be the germ of an entirely new one that transcends and embraces the originating worldviews. Although this happens all the time, when it happens, it is rarely if ever recognized as a process of leadership—because, as discussed before, there is no knowledge principle yet by which such occurrences can be so recognized. Let me give some examples and then deal with the problem of how to make sense of them as leadership.

Johannes Kepler and Tycho Brahe, each making sense of the planets from differing perspectives (Kepler mathematically, Brahe observationally), keep talking until Brahe's observational worldview and Kepler's mathematical worldview create a new way to understand planetary motion, in which it turns out that the old conversation about how to account for retrograde motion was really about elliptical orbits (the new subject) all along.

Supporters of a centralized government and supporters of states' rights keep talking across these worldviews and construct a subject called federalism, in which the old conversation about the potential abuse of central power and the weakness of decentralized power brings into being a new subject called the balance of power. (Sometimes the new subject combines aspects of the old worldviews in new ways and may be framed as a compromise, but not all compromises involve the creation of a new subject; some are simply ways to reassert the existing perspectives in relation to one another.)

The classical worldview of Newtonian physics keeps asserting its powerful truths in factual experiments and yet cannot shed light into another worldview that sees something called the black body problem as a fundamental challenge to classical principles. This conversation breathtakingly creates new subjects called relativity and quantum mechanics, in which it turns out that the old conversation wasn't so much about time and space or particles and waves as it was about space-time and quanta.

Old Master painters take as their subjects mythological figures and religious themes and work within a worldview of representing metaphorically such themes as the evil of greed or the goodness of Mary. Against this worldview the Impressionists argue for art as a way to capture what is right before their eyes—sun and clouds and women swirling parasols. This conversation between worldviews takes an unexpected turn by creating a new subject: nonrepresentational (modern) art, in which it turns out that the old conversation wasn't about what to represent but whether to represent anything at all.

These are rather grand historical examples of what I mean by a conversation across worldviews creating a new subject, which sometimes ends up being the first truth of a whole new worldview. More familiar contemporary examples include the interaction between traditional and feminist views of women, dominant and minority perspectives on the meaning of race, absolute and relative interpretations of the Constitution, liberal and conservative ways of understanding the role of government, and on and on. Any of these conversations might produce some new subject that would transform the terms, reconstruct the reality, and recompose the truths of the participating worldviews. An example of this that may be happening as I write is the creation of a new subject in the conversation across conservationist and economic development worldviews, a subject called sustainable development. If this is an example of the kind of new subject I mean, we will see in the next few years a change in the way both developers and conservationists view their worlds.

One way that these examples could be related to leadership is by understanding certain of the individuals involved as leaders. Thus, we might think of Kepler as a leader or Einstein. We think of America's founding fathers as leaders. When we think this way, we tend to see the emergence of a new subject as something originating in the mind of some person (Johannes Kepler, Ben Franklin) and then given to or expressed to others. This is, of course, the individual way of thinking about leadership that we have discussed as personal dominance and interpersonal influence. This way of thinking works fine *as an explanation* if there is clearly a person who comes up with the new subject (Einstein) but doesn't work when there is not a single person (modern art). Also, while the first or second principle can offer a post hoc *explanation* of such occurrences when there is a clear person to so designate, it cannot offer a way to promote or support the emergence of such new subjects: we know we can't make someone have an idea like the one Einstein had.

Developing a third principle, on the other hand, can help us learn how to promote and support the creation of new subjects.

Instead of understanding Einstein as the autonomous originator of relativity, if we look at the ways in which the new subject called relativity was the result of Einstein's (and a lot of other people's) participation in an ongoing interaction, conversation, across world-views, we could see that what Einstein managed to do was *change the subject* of the conversation. Changing the subject of an ongoing conversation gives us a completely different way to think about creativity, new ideas, and the production of new worldviews from conversations across existing ones. A person can only change the subject of a conversation from inside it, while deeply immersed in it with others; changing the subject means knowing what the subject is now, where it might be headed, how changing it might make it head in more productive directions. Changing the subject is not an individual action, it is an action that can only take place in a context of conversation, a relational context. Changing the subject is a relational way to think about leadership across worldviews.

Such a new subject need not, as in many of the examples chosen thus far, create a new worldview, but may only modify existing world-views. Let me try to give an example of how this might happen.

Many college athletes, basketball players, say, have become increasingly confrontational during competition, getting in their opponents' faces. I am imagining that there is a whole kind of sense about this practice that includes reasons, codes, justifications, values, internal criticisms, facts, and truths. In short, this getting-in-your-face is a worldview or an aspect of some larger worldview (for example, urban playground basketball). There is, of course, a different worldview about all of this, one we might term traditional sportsmanship, that views such behavior as bad form. These two worldviews have some work in common because coaches, players, and spectators make sense of sports from both worldviews. There has been a conversation of the kind I am talking about going on for a number of years across these worldviews. Then, along comes a thirty-second promotional ad produced by and promoting ESPN, the all sports cable channel. Many athletes watch ESPN, and some aspire to be featured on SportsCenter, the sports news show that is the mainstay of that cable channel. The ad shows ESPN Sports-Center announcers, admired and watched by millions of athletes and spectators, getting in the face of, taunting, and generally being verbally abusive to some little kids while playing basketball with them. It is a spectacle that asks a question of everyone who views it. If getting in the face of little kids strikes us as an ugly spectacle, why? Is it because it is bad sportsmanship to act like this anytime? (The answer perhaps from one perspective.) Or is it the difference in age, strength, status? (Perhaps an answer from the other perspective.) If it is bad sportsmanship anytime, why is this worse? Does that mean if the players were more equal it would be more acceptable? And if it is bad because of the difference in age and power, how then is an adult taunting a kid different from an athlete on a very good team taunting an athlete on a not-so-good team? At what point does taunting become OK? The spot seems to pose an inquiry into the conversation across worldviews, equally questioning the assumptions and sensemaking of both, but also respecting and appreciating the assumptions and sensemaking of both. It is thus an inquiry that could just as well result in some further sense being made of taunting as it could in further supporting traditional good sportsmanship. It is an inquiry that seems to take a step in the direction of a new subject, as yet unnamed, but subtly emerging, a code of sportsmanship that recognizes the inclusion of inner-city playground basketball's codes and ways into a changing sense of traditional sportsmanship.

The person (or persons or even a TV network) who manages to change the subject of a conversation across worldviews might then be understood as a leader, even as *the* leader. As the conversation heads off in its new direction, who better to help people take the first steps in that direction? But this kind of leader is also an equal participant in the construction of that conversation (the new worldview) and cannot claim dominance or any special capacity to encompass and relativize other perspectives. This kind of leader cannot create leadership, but must be created by leadership, by the relational dialogue processes between worldviews.

But whether a particular leader is created in this process or not, the leadership tasks become approachable, if not immediately accomplishable. Once there is a new subject constitutive of more than one worldview, some direction meaningful to differing worldviews can be articulated. Once there is a new subject, there is a meaningful something (or someone) for people to commit to. Once there is a new subject, adaptive challenges can begin to be understood in terms of this new subject; that is, common sense across worldviews can be made.

To begin to approach the leadership tasks as if they can be accomplished across worldviews, to begin to search for some subject as yet unknown within differing worldviews, people holding the differing views must begin to take their own view as an object for reflection. Instead of seeing *with* their worldview, assuming that the world is as they understand it to be, people will need to begin to see *through* their worldviews, understand them as useful, sensemaking, and truth giving, but incomplete, not the whole of reality. People thus become aware that how they see the world has built-in limits. Only then can people discover ways in which other worldviews may complement their own—provide some missing pieces of reality, as it were. When differing worldviews begin to engage in this kind of conversation, an entirely new subject (and potentially a new worldview) becomes possible. This new subject will be some form of unity embracing diversity, and it will bring with it the means for accomplishing the leadership tasks.

### All Leadership Is a Process of Shared Meaning-Making

From the truths organized and made sense of by this third leadership principle, it is understood that all leadership is a shared process of relational sense- and meaning-making. All leadership is shared leadership, even the most heroic brand of personal dominance. Dominance is re-viewed as a fact created relationally. A dominant person, from this new view, is not dominant simply by virtue of personal capacity but as a result of participating in a relational community that understands and constructs this dominance. We hinted at this in our discussion of how Mr. Karl was able to be so effective. An effective personally dominant leader is the product of a shared understanding of the first principle. Talking about a relational sense- and meaning-making process is another way to talk about the first principle. The first principle is a way that a whole community has of knowing and recognizing leadership. All of this goes for the second principle as well and for the interpersonally influential leader. That leader too is created through a process of relational participation.

Thus, from the perspective of leadership afforded by this third principle, leadership overall may be re-viewed. If a person is not a leader simply on his or her own but as a result of participation in some relational process, then we have a new and potentially powerful tool for recognizing leadership and for making it happen. We need not confine ourselves to teaching, training, and developing individuals to be or become leaders (although we will want to continue with this as well), we can begin to teach, train, and develop whole communities, whole groups, whole organizations, in how to participate in various leadership processes created from any of the three principles. We can nurture the capacity to recognize leadership in relational interactions and how to make leadership happen, with or without a leader.

Perhaps in this way we can reclaim what we think we have lost. Perhaps we can reclaim the capacity of individuals to lead effectively and powerfully within worldviews while developing the capacity to participate in changing the subject across worldviews. If a person would be a powerful individual leader (a coach, a teacher, a parent, a principal, a manager), let that person understand the way in which he or she must participate relationally in the meaning-making and sensemaking of the team, the class, the family, the school, the department—in short let such leaders see "their" leadership as shared leadership. This could promote and support the development of a whole new cadre of individual leaders within the relational third principle.

At the same time, a third principle organizing the truths I have called relational dialogue may open up a range of possibilities where leadership is concerned that we can only speculate about. New forms of leadership, new approaches and ways of thinking, talking, and acting together will help people work together in a highly diverse world—unity embracing diversity. This way of thinking about all leadership (including dominance and influence) as shared leadership by recognizing leadership as a relational process of sense- and meaning-making is an approach I will call relational leadership.

## The Third Principle and the Leadership Tasks

To repeat the challenge articulated at the beginning of this chapter, which I believe is calling forth a third principle of leadership: When there is shared work among people who make sense of that work and the world from differing worldviews, how can those people accomplish the leadership tasks while holding those differing worldviews as equally worthy and warrantable?

The leadership tasks remain no matter how leadership is understood. Whether a community or organization knows leadership as personal dominance, interpersonal influence, or relational dialogue, the reason for knowing leadership at all is still the need to set direction, create commitment, and face adaptive challenge. How then can the leadership tasks be accomplished from the perspective provided by the third principle?

With the first principle, we saw that the tasks are understood to be accomplishable by the leader alone; with the second principle, we saw how the leader is understood to play a role in accomplishing the tasks through a process of negotiating meaning and influence in the community or organization. From the perspective provided by both the first and second principles, the tasks are accomplished by a leader, although how the leader is understood to do this differs from one principle to the next. Yet both of the first two principles see leadership as a *personal* possession and expression. What are we to make of accomplishing the leadership tasks when leadership is no longer personal but relational? How can direction be set, commitment created, and adaptive challenges faced when no one is personally recognized as the source of leadership? At first this seems to severely limit the power of the third principle. But on closer examination, we can see that the third principle actually expands the possible ways in which leadership can happen and the tasks can be accomplished.

Table 5.1 summarizes how the leadership tasks are approached and accomplished from the perspective provided by each of the three principles.

In this table, boxes with heavy outlines contain the successive principles for knowing leadership and for accomplishing the leadership tasks. Each leadership principle occupies the junction where a way of knowing leadership joins with a way of practicing leadership. In effect a principle is an expression in the form, *I know this as leadership, therefore I recognize leadership when this happens*. We have already discussed in earlier chapters how recognizing leadership is indispensable for accomplishing the leadership tasks: if people do not see that leadership is happening, the tasks cannot even be approached.

The main thing to notice about Table 5.1 is how the range of possible ways of understanding and recognizing leadership increases as new principles develop. Earlier principles are not discarded, they are reinterpreted in light of succeeding principles. This process of reinterpretation is captured in the boxes with light outlines—from the perspective provided by the second principle, the first principle, personal dominance, is reinterpreted as a special case of interpersonal influence in which the leader is understood to have gained special insight into direction, to have the ability to motivate followers, and to create the conditions for facing adaptive challenges. Likewise, from the perspective provided by the third principle, personal dominance is understood as the central participation of the leader in the communal construction of direction, commitment,

Table 5.1  Accomplishing the Leadership Tasks with Three Leadership Principles

| Ways of Understanding Leadership → <br><br> Ways of Practicing Leadership ↓ | Dominance <br> • Leadership happens when a leader acts. | Influence <br> • Leadership happens when a person influences others more than he or she is influenced. | Dialogue <br> • Leadership happens when people make sense together of shared work. |
|---|---|---|---|
| **Personal** <br> • Leadership is a personal endowment of leaders. | **Personal Dominance Principle:** The leader *embodies* direction, *inspires* commitment, and *personally* faces challenges. | Influence is recognized as a *tool* the leader may use to gain agreement or compliance. | Dialogue is recognized as an *intimate approach to communication.* |
| **Interpersonal** <br> • Leadership is a process of negotiating social influence. | The leader *has insight into* direction, *motivates* people to become committed, and *facilitates* the facing of challenges. | **Interpersonal Influence Principle:** A leader *emerges* from *reasoning and negotiating* as the person with the most *influence over direction,* who is thus best able to gain commitment and create the conditions for facing adaptive challenge. | Dialogue is recognized as *perspective taking, reframing, suspending assumptions.* |
| **Relational** <br> • Leadership is meaning-making in communities of practice. | The leader is the *central participant* in the communal construction of direction, commitment, and facing adaptive challenge. | Differences in relative influence *are products of the communal* construction of the meaning of direction, commitment, and facing adaptive challenge. | **Relational Dialogue Principle:** People sharing work create *leadership* by constructing the meaning of direction, commitment, and adaptive challenge. |

and adaptive challenge. *Thus all ways of understanding and recognizing leadership are interpretable from the perspective of the third principle.*

Shaded boxes represent the meaning of future aspects of leadership *before* they are recognized as such. Thus, from the perspective provided by personal dominance, interpersonal influence is a tool while dialogue is recognized as a form of intimate communication. Only as the second principle develops does influence become the cornerstone of leadership, and only as the third principle comes into being does dialogue become recognized as a key aspect of leadership.

Because all ways of understanding and recognizing leadership are interpretable from the perspective of the third principle, the leadership tasks can be understood to be accomplished in a wide range of ways. The CEO of an organization, for example, might be seen as personally dominant, interpersonally influential, and centrally participative in relational dialogue all at the same time. Such multivalent ways of understanding a leader will exist, of course, in the organization or community *as a whole*. Individuals will understand leadership from one perspective or another. Some will see leadership happening when the CEO acts in ways consistent with personal dominance (and will sense a lack of leadership when such behavior is missing), while others will see leadership happening when the CEO engages in processes of negotiating meaning (and will sense a lack of leadership when this is absent and the presence of authoritarianism when the CEO acts dominantly). People in the community or organization who understand leadership from the perspective of the third principle will see leadership happening whenever people are making sense of shared work (and will sense a lack of leadership only if the CEO were to somehow create conditions that block sensemaking). With each succeeding leadership principle, the ways of seeing that leadership is happening increase.

From the perspective of relational dialogue, then, the leadership tasks can be understood to be accomplished in all the ways understood through personal dominance and interpersonal influence, and in addition, the third principle opens the possibility for additional ways to understand the leadership tasks to be accomplished—but only for those people in the organization or community who understand leadership from the perspective provided by the third principle.

Thus, when we talk about shared leadership, for example, as accomplishing the setting of direction by getting the system in the room, or by using open space or search conference technology; and when we talk about people becoming committed to the organization as a whole (not just to an individual leader or to a process of representation through negotiation), we mean that these ways of practicing leadership will be understood *as leadership* only by people who interpret them in the light of the third principle. Other people will see them, perhaps, as no more than inputs to a dominant leader or to a process of negotiating influence.

Leadership development in a community or organization, then, is the process of developing the capacity of the whole to make leadership happen for everyone, no matter how any individual person makes sense of leadership. Small groups might consist entirely of people who make sense of leadership from the third principle; such a group would be able to accomplish the leadership tasks through relational dialogue. Any large, complex community or organization, however, will probably contain people who understand leadership from the perspectives provided by any of the three principles (or perhaps just the first two). Accomplishing the leadership tasks in such an organization can happen only to the extent that all the ways in which leadership is understood to happen are honored. Leadership, in this view, is far from being something that a person can offer independently, simply as an individual, and is seen as a complex construction of multiple levels of meaning.

## Bringing Forth the Third Principle in Communities and Organizations

The way to make leadership better overall in the increasingly complex contexts of the future is to develop the third principle, bring it forth. By developing the third principle I do not mean to follow the model or prescriptions described in this book. This book is no more than an incomplete and only partially articulate attempt to talk about a third principle. Actually developing the third principle means bringing into being in our communities, groups, and organizations *new truths that we take for granted*, a new leadership principle to make a new kind of leadership make sense.

How can people in communities and organizations do this? That is the subject of collaborative inquiry and research my colleagues and I are currently involved in at the Center for Creative Leadership. What follows are some approaches that we are finding promising.

### Cultivate Sensemaking Processes

At the more senior levels in many organizations, teams of managers who used to function in an informational and advisory capacity to the person in charge are these days being called on more and more to work together actively to make sense of what is happening. One senior-management team we collaborated with decided that its monthly operations review meeting was not getting the job done. The members needed to be able to spend time together thinking and talking about strategy for their organization. Facing a rapidly changing environment that was capable of sending shock waves through their business on almost a weekly basis, these managers were finding that getting together once a month for an operational review, while still important, was hardly adequate to their situation. The vice president was determined that his team of direct reports, supplemented by other key managers in the business (numbering around twenty managers total), would learn to "think big" about the business instead of focusing almost exclusively on operational issues.

This kind of change, while it is understandable and almost too obvious, may often be avoided because it is particularly challenging for senior teams. Why? Because it requires a change in mind-set, a change in how meetings are framed, and a change in actual behavior during meetings.

The change in mind-set is from a problem-solving and decision-making mind-set to a sensemaking mind-set. This can be difficult for managers who have been developed and promoted specifically for their ability to solve problems and make decisions. In fact, problem solving and decision making, as key aspects of a manager's job, are often closely associated with the idea of leadership. As we have seen, a personally dominant leader will likely be quite active in this regard, and the interpersonally influential leader will be recognized as being responsible in the end for making decisions. Many managers are practically hardwired to attack problems, discover or create solutions, frame issues that need deciding, make the decisions required, and take responsibility for the outcomes.

This is as it should be *once there is a problem or an issue that needs deciding*. The challenge comes in when the context faced by an organization does not present anything like a problem or issue for decision. Imagine the senior team of a large traditional telecommunications company, for example, facing the environment in telecommunications today. Such a company has been in business for many decades supplying telephone service—phones, lines, switches—and was and still is rooted in equipment, hardware, infrastructure. These are enormous investments and sunk costs. And now, like a sweeping tsunami, new technologies are threatening to render the traditional phone and phone service obsolete. So of course, such a company uses its vast resources to get into the business of wireless communications and supplying backbone for the Internet. It would seem that the problem such an organization faces would be clear, but it is anything but clear. Candidates for problems far outnumber the capacity of any senior team to articulate.

This is a more difficult situation than that of simply needing to agree on a problem statement. What if the managers on a team cannot agree on whether, for example, a competitor's new technology represents a problem? Some see it as a threat while others see it as a distraction best ignored. Or what about the idea that the Internet will soon make free long-distance service a reality? Some see this as a potentially fatal threat, others see it as a fantasy that will never happen, while still others say that even if it happens, it will be more of an opportunity than a threat. Or what about the question of whether the company should stick to the technology side of the Internet, or should become an Internet provider, a portal, what? Perspectives on and ways of framing such issues diverge widely.

This is more like confusion than most managers want to admit. If one suggests to a team of senior managers that they are confused, some readily agree while others feel insulted, so they can't even agree on whether they are confused or not, much less on whether they are threatened with extinction, on the verge of great success, or somewhere in between. Such a context cannot be faced with a problem-solving or decision-making framework because no one knows what the problem is, if there is a problem, or what to do about whatever it is. As Karl Weick (1995) has helped us understand, sensemaking is what is required.

So the change in mind-set involves being able to recognize and acknowledge contexts requiring sensemaking as a prerequisite for going on to problem solving and decision making.

Because sensemaking is a process of exploring the way out of confusion, a meeting with a goal of making sense requires that the normal approach to meetings be reframed. The normal problem-solving and decision-making meeting is designed to move through an agenda of problems-to-be-solved and decisions-to-be-taken. It generally tries to make good use of time, not spend too much time on one thing, get through the agenda, reach an agreed-on conclusion with clear action items and deliverables for the next meeting.

None of these elements are useful in a sensemaking meeting. For one thing, an agenda is virtually useless because the whole idea is to take the conversation where it needs to go, and no one can know where that is in advance. There is no guarantee that the time spent will be productively spent (if by that you mean some prearranged outcome will be reached) because no one knows in advance what outcomes are possible. Agreement is not a goal. Arguing successfully for one's point of view is not a goal. Having people know what to do next is not a goal. Action items will be missing.

So what is sensemaking and what is the goal of meetings that have sensemaking as their reason for being? The goal is to invent, construct, create some way of thinking and talking about what is happening (in the environment, in the organization, on the team) that people can hold in common. The idea is to learn a language—a language consisting of words, ideas, perspectives, feelings—that allows people to know what they agree and disagree about and why, to know what is and is not a problem, what does and does not need deciding. It is a search for shared understanding (which is not the same as agreement) on which the hard work of problem solving and decision making can be built. People on a team will know when their sensemaking has been successful because most of them, if not all, will no longer be confused. They will have some basis for action that is commonly understood. Of course, in a rapidly changing competitive environment, this common sense may be called into question frequently and so sensemaking will become an ongoing process along with the more familiar processes of problem solving and decision making.

Changing mind-sets about the nature of work and reframing meetings to call forth a group's sensemaking capacity will also require changes in how people behave in meetings, specifically in how they talk to one another.

### Explore Narrative Modes of Understanding

One key change is to introduce the narrative mode of thinking and talking into meetings. Mostly managers rely on the mode of understanding by analysis. Analysis takes the world apart and asks, What is this thing composed of, and what are its constituent parts? For example, if sales are lagging, the analytical mode suggests looking at the parts: regions, products, markets, trends, figures and breakdowns of figures and sometimes breakdowns of the breakdowns. This is perfectly reasonable and often quite effective. It approaches understanding by taking the object to be understood apart, breaking down its complexities into more manageable and digestible pieces. Yet we have all experienced something of the mind-numbing potential of analysis: What, exactly, does all this tell us? We want to know.

This is where the narrative mode of understanding can come in. If the analytical mode is especially useful for solving problems and making decisions, the narrative mode can be especially useful for making sense. Where the analytical mode takes things apart, the narrative mode tells about how things hang together. Sales are lagging? What's the story? Telling a story about lagging sales means coming up with a plot that explains the results you are looking at. It means expressing something of the cause-and-effect relationships overall. It means having a sense of where sales were and where they are going as a way of understanding where they are now.

The useful thing about using narrative modes of understanding is that they are remarkably open to sensemaking. We know that any explanation of something like lagging sales will be questioned, doubted. The problem with the analytical mode is that if one wants to question the explanation, one must deal with a mass of analytical detail, subparts, complex interrelations, assumptive bases, and so forth. By contrast, if one is doubtful about a story that has just been told about lagging sales, it can be much easier to finger just where the doubt comes in, just where the story stops making sense. Better yet, anyone can offer a quick alternative story. Numerous stories purporting to explain the sales figures can be offered, compared, considered, appreciated, critiqued, revised. Pieces of one story can be grafted on another story to make a new story. By staying with the narrative mode, people are staying with the whole meaning and not getting bogged down in analysis.

### Develop the Capacity for Dialogue

Dialogue is a charged word. It is something that many organization development professionals have been trying to get managers to learn how to do for some forty years at least—with, I think, no more than modest success. From what I know (which is surely incomplete here) the main idea behind dialogue has been that getting along competently on an interpersonal level and having respect for one another as human beings is critical for working together well. The assumption has been that managers should use dialogue in meetings because the meeting will go better, people will have more genuine respect and liking for one another, and will understand one another better. I agree with all of these goals in the sense that they are goals I find worthy, but I suggest that they are not sufficiently meaningful to most managers to get them to make what amounts to difficult and profound changes in the way they talk. I suspect that most managers think they get along with their fellow managers and respect them just about enough as things are and getting into dialogue is an unnecessary burden. They have too much else on their plates, thank you.

This attitude to dialogue will be changing. Dialogue is not an add-on, not a way to enhance the work environment anymore. It has become critical. First of all, if any of what I have said about the emergence of a third principle makes sense, then dialogue becomes necessary simply because, in the same way that exhortation and command is the language of the first principle and persuasion and argument is the language of the second, dialogue is the language of the third. So dialogue seems more like a strategic imperative for most organizations than an aspect of improved climate.

Dialogue is both relatively easy to do and quite difficult. On a behavioral level, we have had success in getting people to talk to one another using principles of dialogue by simply using images as mediators of conversation. In fact, we are exploring the notion that many ordinary conversations people have every day are much closer to dialogue than most people recognize. Whenever people talk about something they have each experienced *with the goal of learning the other person's experience* (So, what did you think of the movie?), we are speculating dialogue, or something close to it, may be the mode of conversation. We have come to this speculation because of the complete ease with which all kinds of people can engage in something very like dialogue by simply having them talk about images following certain simple rules. This seems to be something that people already know how to do and actually find enjoyable. The rub comes, as a number of participants in this activity have pointed out, when dialogue is attempted under conditions of stress, competition, conflict, where there will be winners and losers. This is how dialogue gets very difficult.

If dialogue is defined as a mutual search for a new understanding through face-to-face conversation, all the parties to dialogue stand to lose at least a part of what is valued and meaningful to them in such a search. Under conditions of stress, conflict, competition, then, dialogue requires more of people than just following some rules of conduct while talking. It requires that people loosen their grip on the certainty of the truths they hold dear, and this can feel like giving up one's beliefs, principles, integrity, and even one's very identity. It requires an openness to a new reality that is unproven, unknown, nothing more than a tenuous try at truth, and this can feel like letting go of what makes sense to grasp something more like nonsense. These are formidable barriers that ask people to function at high levels of personal maturity entailing a paradoxical mix of confidence and humility, strength of will and willingness to bend, belief in self and acknowledgment of limits, the courage of one's convictions and doubting all conviction. Such, however, is the challenge of an emerging third principle.

### Increase Personal Responsibility for Leadership

The most frequent (and deeply felt) objection to the idea of a third leadership principle, to relational dialogue as a way of creating leadership, is born of the conclusion that relational dialogue takes the individual out of leadership and reduces individual responsibility. As the saying goes, if we make everyone responsible, don't we wind up with no one responsible?

A closer look at the three principles, however, reveals that in the movement from the first to the second to the third, personal responsibility for leadership increases. It may seem paradoxical, but as the idea that leadership is a personal achievement is increasingly called into question from principle to principle, personal responsibility increases. I see no paradox at all. The whole point of the first principle is for a leader to take personal responsibility for leadership, leaving followers responsible only for being good followers. It is the very idea (bordering on a demand) that followers have more responsibility for leadership that is a key driver of the movement away from the first and toward the second principle. It is the second principle that introduces the idea that followers play a significant reciprocal role in what is still thought of as the leader's leadership. In calling forth a third principle of leadership that not only does not require a leader, but redefines the meaning of the word (no longer a person who creates leadership but a person who is created by leadership), the requirement that many people (if not everyone in a community) take responsibility is also created. With the third principle, it is not merely desirable that many people take responsibility for leadership, it is mandatory. The principle cannot be used to create leadership without this increased personal responsibility.

But, you may say, this is just the problem. When many people are responsible, how do we know whom to hold *accountable?* How can we be sure people are not loafing, failing to take responsibility and hoping not to be noticed because so many others are taking responsibility? And if everyone begins to think that way (as it is only human nature to do) is it not true that you end up with no one taking responsibility?

These are critically important questions in the emergence of a third leadership principle. In my experience it is questions such as these that create a great deal of confusion about so-called shared leadership, distributed leadership, and throw a lot of cold water on the attempt to make more people in an organization act like leaders.

In the first place, it is useful to make a distinction between responsibility and accountability. As parents, we should feel responsible, for example, for the safety of all children in our community, but we need not feel accountable for a child who has been injured as a result of another parent's carelessness. Feeling responsible for doing what it is within our power to do is not the same as being held accountable for all specific outcomes. This is a key differ-ence between a person who has authority and the idea of a third principle of leadership that is being articulated here. From the per-spective afforded by the third principle, accountability is an aspect of the system of authority. Leadership is certainly not disconnected from this system of authority, but neither is it identical to that system. Responsibility for leadership, then, is not the same as accountability for results. A person could feel deeply responsible for playing a role in accomplishing the leadership tasks without being held account-able for all outcomes. If, on the other hand, a manager who is being held accountable for results frames this as also being personally responsible for leadership as well, that is an understanding of leader-ship by the light of the first or second principle, not the third.

Second, people can only take responsibility for that which they understand is within their power to do something about. There are many parents in every community who are powerless (or just feel powerless) to do anything at all about the safety of all children. They may struggle with taking responsibility for their own chil-dren. Whether we see them as loafing or lacking capacity, they are not able to take responsibility beyond their immediate sphere of action. The same is true in organizations, and that is why the first principle remains an important, vital aspect of leadership. Its logic enables a single person to take responsibility for leadership on behalf of many. The second principle enables more people to take some responsibility for leadership while still recognizing that some-one is more responsible for leadership than anyone else. The third principle, in seeking to create meaning across worldviews, affords a perspective in which everyone is an equal partner in creating lead-ership and accomplishing the leadership tasks. This may have im-plications for the system of accountability, but it does not require that accountability be diluted to the point of vanishing.

This sense of developmental movement from the first to second to an emerging third principle offers a new way to think about lead-ership development at the level of a whole system. Instead of seek-ing to develop leadership by developing individual leaders, this way of looking at leadership—as an unfolding of ever more involving and complex knowledge principles—helps us see how leadership can be developed as a systemic capacity: the capacity of a system to accomplish leadership tasks at various levels of complexity, bringing in increasing numbers of increasingly responsible people. The goal of leadership development in an organization could thus be to increase the capacity of the whole system to make sense of direction, commitment, and adaptive challenges at all relevant levels of understanding and responsibility. This would not be done by simply training people in positions of authority (or even people with the potential for such positions in the future) in precepts of effective leadership. Instead, the goal of leadership development would be for everyone, from entry-level operational employees on through first-line supervisors, middle managers, directors, vice presidents, and the top managers to construct a sense of what responsibility for leadership is appropriate and useful, how such a responsibility is carried out within their interrelationships in the organization, and when they should be expected to enlarge their sense of responsibility for leadership. Such an approach to leadership development at this systemic level would recognize at least three distinct knowledge principles organizing three sets of truths about leadership.

*Epilogue*

# A New World for Zoffner Music

It was Elena who worried the most about the failure of Project X. Questions haunted her. Why had they not been able to go forward? Why had the two divisions of Zoffner Music not been able to work together? Why did it seem that they were trapped within their differing ways of thinking about the new instrument? Was she the only person in the organization who appreciated both the traditional and the digital instruments? The only one who wanted to find the best of both worlds?

The fallout from the project reverberated for months, stretching into years. Musitron went ahead with an advanced keyboard with some of the features of the Project X instrument, but of course without the analog aspects, the real strings and hammers. This product gave the division a lift in the market for a while, but it was a market jammed with competing offerings, and Musitron's share stayed relatively small. Zoffner Piano went back to making traditional pianos. Unwilling (and truth to tell, unable) to compromise on quality, its prices inched up, slowly but surely pushing it toward the market dominated by instruments with more prestigious names.

Everyone on both sides of the divide, Elena suspected, was relieved to be back home among colleagues they could talk to without too much confusion or irresolute disagreement.

One day more than a year after the falling out, Eddie commented to Elena, "I guess it's always a good idea for people to just stick to what they do best."

"But, Eddie, what if what we do best is taking us in the wrong direction? What if all the experience and expertise of the past is becoming irrelevant?"

"If the piano becomes irrelevant," Eddie replied with some heat, "I don't want to live to see it!"

"I don't mean the piano, Eddie, I mean our piano, the Zoffner piano. We know already it's not what it once was. Already it's too expensive for a working family to afford. The family that bought my father's piano is buying a digital keyboard now, and it's not even ours they're buying. I'm afraid it won't be long, Eddie, and we won't have any customers for the piano or the keyboard. The piano will still be relevant, but we won't."

Eddie turned pale. It had apparently never hit him quite like that.

Raul was at this time much more concerned about Musitron than the overall company. Privately he was convinced that Zoffner Piano's days were numbered and that Musitron was the way forward for the company. He was determined to turn the digital keyboard business around before the piano business began to lose money. He quietly lobbied Elena to put more and more of the piano business's dwindling profits into R&D in the digital business. Elena saw his reasoning but found the idea of milking her father's legacy to support the development of Musitron unsettling.

She was torn. She couldn't sleep nights. She lost her appetite. Finally she went to see her father and poured out all her troubles to him. It was with such a feeling of relief that she told him about everything as he listened intently. He would know what to do. When Elena was done talking, Karl blinked at her.

"What are you doing here telling me all this? You think I want to know about things like this? The end of my company? You think I can save it? The day is past for that, long past."

"But Father . . . " Elena was thunderstruck by this rejection. He waved his hand at her, as if to stop her tears.

"Have you talked to Nan about this?" he asked matter-of-factly. "She used to have some peculiar ideas she would throw out to me. Maybe what you need right now is one of her peculiar ideas."

So it happened that the beginning of a new era at Zoffner Music began with a peculiar idea from its oldest—and some said its stodgiest—employee, Nan in finance. Here is what she had to say to Elena when Elena finally got around to asking her.

"We never have in this company understood who our customer is. Do you have any idea? No, I doubt it. You think it's the fathers and mothers who buy our pianos or the kids who play them. But we always knew in the old days that this wasn't really our customer. This was the person who bought the piano, maybe, but the person who told the fathers and mothers which piano to buy was the piano teacher. Don't look so surprised. Think about it. You're a mother and you want your ten-year-old daughter to take piano. What do you do? Go out and buy a piano? No. You go to a piano teacher and you talk about lessons. How much, how often, how much time, is she too old to start, too young? Then you ask the teacher, 'What kind of piano should I buy?' And the piano teacher says, 'I recommend a Zoffner.' She says this because the Zoffner is affordable. She doesn't want to lose a student because the mother and father can't afford the piano. She also says this because the Zoffner has enough quality craftsmanship that once the child begins to learn to play, the piano will keep up, and so will the lessons. To make a long story short, piano teachers like Zoffners because this is the piano that increases their business."

Elena practically shot out of her seat, propelled by a sudden insight into what needed to happen.

In future times the week would be known as the week that wasn't. This was because Elena stopped production in both Zoffner Piano and Musitron, shut down the plants, reduced work to its absolute minimum, so that everyone in the company who wished to do so could attend a week-long retreat she somewhat fancifully named The Search for Our New World. If you didn't want to spend the week in this search, you got the time off, no questions asked. Almost everyone showed up, however. Many people were simply curious. At a deeper level, they sensed this was going to be big, and they wanted to be there to see it.

They started each day at their regular time and quit each day at quitting time. They convened in various places around the two plants. Chairs were moved out of offices, places were cleared, people sat on the floor, leaning against the wall. Zoffner employees and Musitron employees mixed, a little uncomfortably to be sure, but that was over by the end of the week.

What were they doing? Basically they were doing what Nan had done: telling what they knew to anyone who would listen, and if no one would listen, they were listening to other people talk about what they knew. There were only three rules:

• You had to make yourself understood to your listeners, who could show they didn't understand by simply waving their hands. This was a bit awkward at first, but by midweek people were waving their hands freely and speakers were working hard to stop them from waving. A programmer from Musitron said later that he never knew how much jargon and how many acronyms he used as a matter of habit. It was like learning to speak an entirely new language to make himself understood to nontechnical people, but it was a very useful language.

• *Whatever you talked about had to be something you believed was important to the future of Zoffner Music, Zoffner Piano, or Musitron.* Beyond that there were no restrictions on content. People talked about technology and markets and working conditions and problems with suppliers, but they also talked about how things had changed, what made them happy and unhappy, and what their dreams were for the future.

• *If you were listening, you couldn't talk, only wave your hand to indicate you didn't understand.* Sometimes a group of listeners was as small as one or two; sometimes there were twenty or more listening, waving their hands from time to time, but otherwise just listening, knowing that if they had something to say, they needed to form up their own group of listeners. You posted your topic on the bulletin board and people either showed up or didn't to listen to what was on your mind. Between these presentation sessions there were hour-long breaks where people could talk freely to one another and simply socialize.

*It was a kind of a search conference, open space, free-for-all, social, and picnic all rolled into one. For three days they did nothing else. At the end of the first day many people doubted there would be the energy or the need to go for the full three days. But by the middle of the third day, people were seeing that they had more to say to one another than there would ever be time for.*

*The fourth day was the day in which they would attempt to create a shared sense of the future. People formed into cross-functional* teams with the mission of telling a story that would reveal something important about this future. Each team was presented with the beginning of a plot, a big opportunity or a terrible problem or an unexpected event. The point was to tell what would happen next and why and how it would all come out. When the people on the story teams disagreed about the plot of the story, they were encouraged to try to build their disagreement into their story. Let the conflict drive the plot forward. Each team had to be able to tell its story to the other teams later, and so they were supplied with butcher paper, colored markers, magazines, scissors, paste, and a variety of supplies to bring their story to life visually, a kind of illustrated book or movie of the story. Each story team named their book or movie and presented it to the others. After each such showing of a story there was time for question and answer, conversation and exploration.

On the last day, people were challenged to find as many others as they could who shared with them some vision of the future. They were to use whatever means they could to form groups of people as large as possible who could express some coherent future vision that each person in the group could claim as his or her own. The goal was by the end of the day to know how many possible visions of the future there were within Zoffner Music that a fairly large number of people could claim and what those visions were. No one knew how this would turn out. Would there be dozens of visions with perhaps only ten or twelve people claiming each? Or would there be far fewer, visions capable of being owned by scores, even hundreds of people? And what would the visions be like, how would they speak about the future? There was no set way for people to make themselves part of a vision group. Some people, using the technique of the first three days, advertised a potential vision on the bulletin board. Others went in search of a group they could join.

In the end, to the amazement of everyone, not least Elena herself, it came out like this: many visions with small groups of claimants worked their way down to three with large groups of people claiming one of the three. Not one of these three groups was made up of only Zoffner Piano or Musitron employees. All three of the final visions were about a future in which Zoffner Piano and Musitron would somehow work together.

The members of the leadership council took these three visions, which were remarkably detailed and fleshed out in story form as real narratives of a new world, and began their own conversation, their own process of making sense of the future. When they finally arrived at a common sense of their future, they presented it to the assembled company, saying, in effect, "What if—?" And the company said, "Yes, let's do."

So Elena found out that leadership was something she was good at after all. It wasn't her father's leadership, and it wasn't even her leadership, but it couldn't have happened without her. She, along with everyone else in the deep blue sea, was the one indispensable individual.

# Bibliography

Bass, B. M. *Bass & Stogdill's Handbook of Leadership*. New York: Free Press, 1990.

Basseches, M. *Dialectical Thinking and Adult Development*. Norwood, N.J.: Ablex, 1984.

Bruner, J. S. *Acts of Meaning*. Cambridge, Mass.: Harvard University Press, 1990.

Cooperrider, D. "Positive Imagery, Positive Action." In S. Srivastva, D. Cooperrider, and Associates, *Appreciative Management and Leadership: The Power of Positive Thought and Action in Organizations*. San Francisco: Jossey-Bass, 1990.

Drath, W. H. "Approaching the Future of Leadership Development." In C. D. McCauley, R. S. Moxley, and E. Van Velsor (Eds.), *The Center for Creative Leadership Handbook of Leadership Development*. San Francisco: Jossey-Bass, 1998.

Drath, W. H., and Palus, C. J. *Making Common Sense: Leadership as Meaning-Making in a Community of Practice*. Greensboro, N.C.: Center for Creative Leadership, 1994.

Follett, M. P. *Dynamic Administration: The Collected Papers of Mary Parker Follett*. New York: HarperCollins, 1942.

Gergen, K. J. *The Saturated Self: Dilemmas of Identity in Contemporary Life*. New York: Basic Books, 1991.

Gergen, K. J. *Realities and Relationships*. Cambridge, Mass.: Harvard University Press, 1994.

Goodman, N. *Ways of Worldmaking*. Indianapolis, Ind.: Hackett, 1978.

Heifetz, R. *Leadership Without Easy Answers*. Cambridge, Mass.: Harvard University Press, 1994.

Kegan, R. *The Evolving Self*. Cambridge, Mass.: Harvard University Press, 1982.

Kegan, R. *In Over Our Heads*. Cambridge, Mass.: Harvard University Press, 1994.

Lambert, L., and Associates. *The Constructivist Leader*. New York: Teachers College Press, 1995.

Palus, C. J., and Drath, W. H. *Evolving Leaders: A Model for Promoting Leadership*

*Development in Programs.* Greensboro, N.C.: Center for Creative Leadership, 1995.

Rost, J. C. *Leadership for the Twenty-First Century.* New York: Praeger, 1991.

Weick, K. E. *Sensemaking in Organizations.* Thousand Oaks, Calif.: Sage, 1995.

Wenger, E. *Communities of Practice.* Cambridge, U.K.: Cambridge University Press, 1998.

# Index

**A**

Accountability, 163–164
Acting with followers, 69–71
Actions and thoughts, as ways of recognizing leadership, 4–7, 27–28, 35
Adaptive challenge, facing (leadership task): diversity and, 109–110; interpersonal influence and, 25, 87–89, 90, 107–108, 109–110; interpersonal influence limitations for, 109–110; issues addressed by, 21–22; overview of, 18–19, 21–22; personal dominance limitations for, 53–55, 56; in personal dominance principle, 24, 42–44; relational dialogue and, 26; routine challenges versus, 21, 42; in Zoffner case study, 42–44, 53–54
Agenda, 158
Alignment: commitment and, 20–21; commitment and, in interpersonal influence principle, 87
Allport, F. H., 8–9
Ambiguity, possibility of, in interpersonal influence principle, 85–86, 90, 113
American communities, limiting contexts in, to interpersonal influence, 100–102
American founding fathers, 146
Analysis mode of understanding, 159; narrative mode versus, 159–160
Anger, 137
"Anything goes" philosophy, 142–143
Art, 145
Assimilation, 125, 126

**B**

Bacon, R., 58
Balance of power, 145

Bass, B. M., 10
Black body problem, 145
Boundary issues, 118–124
Brahe, T., 145
Bureaucratic hierarchy, 105

**C**

Case study. See Zoffner Piano Company
Center for Creative Leadership, 156
Centralized government, 145
Challenge, adaptive. See Adaptive challenge, facing (leadership task)
Change. See Adaptive challenge; Organizational change
Charisma, dominance and, 65–66
Chief executive officer (CEO), personal dominance perspective on, 37–38
City council example, 127
Coercion, 37, 71, 72
Cohesion, 20
Collaborative learning, 14–15
Collaborative relationships, with suppliers and customers, 103–104
College athletes, 147–148
Commitment, creating and maintaining (leadership task): direction setting and, 41; diversity and, 109, 117–118; interpersonal influence and, 24–25, 86–87, 90, 109; interpersonal influence limitations for, 109, 110, 117–118; issues addressed by, 20–21; overview of, 18–19, 20–21; personal dominance limitations for, 52–53, 56; in personal dominance principle, 23, 40–42; relational dialogue and, 25–26; in Zoffner case study, 41–42, 52–53

Communities, American, 100–102

Community change, adaptive challenge and, 22, 24, 25. *See also* Adaptive challenge

Community citizen committee example, 128

Competitiveness, 118

Complexity: and direction setting under interpersonal influence principle, 85, 87; and direction setting under personal dominance principle, 50–51, 85

Conflict: mutual acknowledgment of shared work in, 129–131, 132; relational dialogue approaches and, 155–165

Confusion: adaptive challenge and, 21–22; personal dominance principle and, 42; sensemaking and, 158

Conservationist worldview, 146

Construction of reality: through relational processes, 135–165. *See also* Relational dialogue; Worldviews

*Constructivist Leader, The* (Lambert), 108

Contexts: of limits to interpersonal influence, 98–110; of limits to personal dominance, 47–55, 65–66, 97; that call for relational dialogue, 125–134; writers about, 107–108

Conversation among worldviews, 144–149, 160–162. *See also* Relational dialogue

Cooperation, personal dominance principle and, 38

Coordination, commitment and, 20–21

Copernicus, 67

Creating and maintaining commitment. *See* Commitment, creating and maintaining (leadership task)

Cross-divisional teams, 96–97, 103–104

Cross-functional teams, 104, 111–124

Cultural differences (international or ethnic), 29, 98–100, 106, 130, 131

Cultural differences (organizational), 95–96, 105–107; in cross-divisional teams, 103–104; in cross-functional teams, 103–104, 112–124; supplier and customer partnerships and, 103–104

Customer definition, 169–170

Customer orientation, 130

Customers, collaborative relationships with, 103–104

**D**

Decentralization, 145

Decision-making versus sensemaking mind-set, 157–159

Definitions: of leadership, 8–10; principles versus, 7–10

Democracy, rise of, 90

Dependence, 36, 39

Depth psychology worldview, 143

Dialogue, relational. *See* Relational dialogue

Dialogue capacity, 160–162

Dialogue rules, 170–171

Differences: in American communities, 100–102; as aspects of leadership, 81; assimilation of, in personal dominance principle, 125, 126; in cross-functional, self-managed team, 112–124; cultural (international or ethnic), 29, 98–100, 106, 130, 131; cultural (organizational), 95–96, 103–104, 105–107; integration of, in interpersonal influence principle, 79–81, 85–88, 91–92, 95–96, 106–107, 125–126; leader as repository for, in interpersonal influence principle, 80–81, 85–86, 91–92, 108; learning from, 107; limitations of interpersonal influence and, 98–104; negotiation of, in interpersonal influence principle, 78–84, 86–87, 95–96, 125–126; in organizations, 103–104. *See also* Diversity; Perspectives; Worldviews

Differing worldviews. *See* Differences; Perspectives; Worldviews

Direction setting (leadership task): creating commitment and, 41; diversity and, 109, 116–117; interpersonal influence limitations for, 109, 110; in interpersonal influence principle, 84–86, 90, 109, 116–117; overview of, 18–20; personal dominance limitations for, 50–51, 56; in personal dominance principle, 23, 39–40; questions addressed by, 19–20; in Zoffner case study, 39–40, 51

Diversity: in American communities, 100–102; globalization and, 98–100;

as limiting context for interpersonal influence principle, 102–110; in organizations, 106–107; relational dialogue and, 151; unity embracing, 98–100, 106–107, 108–110, 113–115; unity masking, 116–124
Dominance, 32–33, 72. *See also* Personal dominance
Doubt, openness to, in interpersonal influence principle, 79–80, 85–87

**E**

Economic development worldview, 146
EgyptAir Flight 990 calamity, 99–100, 128
Einstein, A., 146, 147
Emotions, 137
Enlightenment, age of, 58, 90
Equal worth of differing worldviews, 131–132, 139, 142–143
ESPN SportsCenter, 147–148
Exploitation, 41–42, 52–53

**F**

Facing adaptive challenge. *See* Adaptive challenge, facing (leadership task)
Federalism, 145
Feminism, 146
First leadership principle. *See* Personal dominance
Flattened organization, 103, 104–107
Followers, under interpersonal influence principle: acting with versus on, 69–71; commitment of, 86–87; leaders versus, 68–69, 89–90, 92; motives of, 69–71; reciprocity of leader and, 108
Followers, under personal dominance principle: dependence of, 36, 39, 47–49; exploitation of, 41–42, 52–53; loss of, 48, 54–55; loyalty of, 41–42, 48, 52–53, 87; psychological development of, 49, 59–60; reciprocity of leader and, 40, 41–42, 43, 48–49, 52–53, 60–61, 65–66
Found reality, relationally constructed reality versus, 139–144
Franklin, B., 146
Functional differences in organizations: limits of interpersonal influence prin-

ciple for, 103–104, 112–124; relational dialogue and, 131–133
Future search conference, in Zoffner case study, 170–173

**G**

Gandhi, M., 37
Gerth, H., 10
Global corporation example, 128
Global interconnection, 126
Globalization, as limiting context for interpersonal influence, 98–100
Gods, personal dominance principle and, 57–58
Goodman, N., 125

**H**

Hegel, G., 70
Heifetz, R., 107–108
Heroic leadership, 37–38
High school faculty example, 128–129
History: of interpersonal influence principle, 90–91; of personal dominance principle, 57–59

**I**

Impressionists, 145
Individual responsibility, 162–165
Influence, as definition of leadership, 9–10, 68–69. *See also* Interpersonal influence
Interaction: construction of reality through, 135–165; leadership defined by, 6–7. *See also* Relational dialogue
Interconnection: as context for relational dialogue, 126–134; existence of, 125–126; of worldviews, 125–165
Interpersonal capacities, 160–162
Interpersonal influence (second leadership principle), 12, 63–92; achievement of, summarized, 91–92; acting with followers' motives and, 69–71; adaptive challenge and, 25, 87–89, 90; capacities and limits of, summarized, 110; capacities of, compared with limits of personal dominance, 84–92, 90; commitment and, 24–25, 86–87, 90; degree of, 68–69; direction setting and, 24, 84–86, 90; emergence of, 77–84, 90–91, 97; historical development of, 90–91; leader as repository

Interpersonal influence, *continued*
for differing perspectives in, 80–81,
85–87, 88, 91–92, 108; leader's perspective as container for negotiation
in, 78, 88; leader's perspective as open
to question and doubt in, 79–80; leaders versus followers in, 68–69, 89–90;
leadership role in, 72; leadership tasks
and, 24–25, 84–90, 153; meaning of,
65–77; negotiation of meaning in,
78–84, 125–126; overview of, 13–14;
personal dominance versus, 13–14, 72,
79–80, 91; relational dialogue versus,
151–154; as shared leadership, 91–92,
101–102, 107–108, 150; social influence and, 67–68; sources of power in,
72; taken-for-granted truths of, 14,
65–77, 97–98, 110; transition from
personal dominance to, 65–67, 71,
73–84; unity embracing diversity and,
98–100, 106–107, 108–110, 113–115;
in Zoffner case study, 63–64, 65–66,
73–77, 78–79, 82–85, 86
Interpersonal influence (second leadership principle) limitations, 93–124; for
adaptive challenge, 109–110; in
American communities, 100–102;
boundary problems and, 118–124; for
commitment, 109, 110, 117–118; contexts of, 98–107; in cross-functional
teams, 111–124; customer relationships and, 103–104; for direction setting, 109, 110, 116–117; diversity and,
98–102, 106–107, 113–122; globalization and, 98–100; knowledge management and, 107; leadership tasks and,
108–115; the learning organization
and, 107; marginalized versus privileged voices and, 100–102; organizational changes and, 102–104; senior
management trends as, 105–106; summary of, 108–110; summary of capacities and, 110; supplier relationships
and, 103–104; trend toward organizing
around work as, 104–107, 108–110;
writers about, 107–108; in Zoffner
case study, 93–97, 111–116, 119–122
Interpersonal relationship: leadership as,
9–10; personal dominance and, 47–49
Intuition, 141
Irish Republicans and Unionists conflict,
128

Islamic worldview, 99–100
Israelis, 98–99, 130

**J**

Judeo-Christian worldview, 100

**K**

Kepler, J., 145, 146
Kings, 57–58
Knowing, ways of, 140–141, 152
Knowledge management, 107
Knowledge principles: definitions versus,
7–10; reciprocity and, 31–32; truth
and, 12; as ways of understanding
leadership, 6–7, 27, 151–154. *See also*
Leadership principles
Kosovo crisis, 130

**L**

Lambert, L., 108
Language for sensemaking, 159
Leaders: as creators of new subjects, 146;
versus followers, under interpersonal
influence principle, 68–69, 89–90, 92;
multivalent ways of understanding,
154; psychological development of,
49; in relational dialogue principle,
133–134, 146; styles of, 10–12
Leadership: definitions of, 8–10; management versus, 21, 80; principles versus
definitions of, 7–10; recognizing, 4–7,
27–28, 150, 152–154; systemic view
of, 26–30
Leadership development: in relational
dialogue principle, 155, 164–165; as
shared process, 61; at whole-system
level, 164–165
Leadership effectiveness, 28
*Leadership for the Twenty-First Century*
(Rost), 107
Leadership principles, 3–18; caveats
about, 28–29; comparative approaches
of, to differing wordviews, 125–126;
cultural differences and, 29; definitions of leadership versus, 7–10; leadership effectiveness and, 28; leadership
styles versus, 10–12; leadership tasks
and, 22–26, 151–154; leadership tasks
and, systemic view of, 26–30; limits of,
importance of, 55–57; overview of,
12–15; primacy of third, 12; recogniz-

ing, 28, 152–154; reinterpretation of, 152, 154; summary of, with leadership tasks, 27, 151–154; in systemic view of leadership, 26–30; universality of, 29; validity of, 29; as ways of recognizing leadership, 4–7, 27–28. *See also* Interpersonal influence (second leadership principle); Personal dominance (first leadership principle); Relational dialogue (third leadership principle)

Leadership styles, 10–12

Leadership tasks, 18–26; in cross-functional, self-managed team, 112–122; interpersonal influence principle and, 24–25, 84–90, 153; leadership principles and, 22–26, 151–154; leadership principles and, systemic view of, 26–30; overview of, 18–22; personal dominance principle and, 23–24, 35–36, 38–46, 50–55, 56, 153; relational dialogue principle and, 25–26, 132–133, 140, 144, 149, 151–155, 153; summary of, with leadership principles, 27, 151–154. *See also* Adaptive challenge, facing (leadership task); Commitment, creating and maintaining (leadership task); Direction setting (leadership task)

Leadership traits, personal dominance perspective and, 36–37, 48

*Leadership Without Easy Answers* (Heifetz), 107–108

Learning organization, 107

Legitimacy, in personal dominance principle, 53–61

Limits of interpersonal influence. *See* Interpersonal influence limitations

Limits of personal dominance. *See* Personal dominance limitations

Living, demands of new form of, 126–134

Loyalty, 41–42, 48, 52–53, 87

**M**

Management versus leadership, 21, 80

Manipulation, 37

Marginalized voices, as limiting context for interpersonal influence, 100–102

Mathematical worldview, 145

Meaning-making, leadership as process of shared, 149–151

Meaning-making principles. *See* Knowledge principles; Leadership principles

Meetings: dialogue in, 160–162; future search, in Zoffner case study, 170–173; sensemaking versus problem-solving, 158–159

Metaphor, 25

Middle East conflict, 98–99, 130

Mills, C. W., 10

Mind-set, problem-solving versus sensemaking, 156–159

Modes of understanding, 159–160

Motives of followers, acting with, 69–71

**N**

Narrative modes of understanding, 25, 159–160

Nation, C., 37

Natural leaders, 1–3, 12–13, 23, 31, 32–36. *See also* Personal dominance

Negotiation: commitment and, 13–14, 24, 86–87; in interpersonal influence principle, 78–84, 86–87, 125–126; leader's perspective as container for, 78, 88; leader's perspective as open to question in, 79–80, 85–87. *See also* Commitment

*New York Times*, 99

Newtonian worldview, 145

**O**

Objective and subjective truth, 67–68, 135–140

Objectivity, 141

Observational worldview, 145

Observer, 67–68

Old Master painters, 145

Open systems, 103, 108

Organizational change: adaptive challenge and, 22, 24, 25; as limiting context for interpersonal influence principle, 102–108; relational dialogue approaches in, 155–165. *See also* Adaptive challenge

Organizing around work, as limiting context for interpersonal influence principle, 104–107, 108–110

**P**

Painters, Old Master and Impressionist, 145

Palestinians, 98–99, 130

Parents: personal dominance principle of, 33, 59; relational construction of, 138; responsibility versus accountability of, 163, 164
Partnerships, 103–104
Paternalism, 37, 59
Performance appraisal, 80
Personal dominance (first leadership principle), 12, 31–61; adaptive challenge and, 24, 42–44, 53–55; assimilation of differences in, 125, 126; capacities and limits of, summarized, 56; charisma and, 65–66; commitment and, 23, 40–42, 52–53; direction setting and, 23, 39–40, 50–51; dominance and, 32–33; expression of, 35; interpersonal influence versus, 13–14, 24, 72, 79–80, 91; leadership tasks and, 23–24, 35–36, 38–46, 50–55, 56, 153; legitimacy and legitimacy failure in, 53–61; letting go of, 82–84; meaning of, 32–38; natural leaders and, 33–34; as natural quality, 32–36; overview of, 12–13; personal element in, 34, 47–48; relational dialogue and, 25, 151–154; replacement of, with interpersonal influence, 65–67, 71, 82–84; as shared leadership, 60–61, 65–66, 149–150; taken-for-granted truths of, 13, 32–36; traits and, 36–37, 48; uniqueness of leaders in, 47–48; in Zoffner case study, 12, 23, 30, 31–32, 35–36, 39–40. See also Followers, under personal dominance principle
Personal dominance (first leadership principle) limitations, 47–61; contexts of, 47–55, 65–66, 97; in creating commitment, 52–53, 56; in facing adaptive challenges, 53–55, 56; historical perspective on, 57–59; importance of understanding, 55–57; interpersonal influence capacities versus, 84–92; loss of leader and, 47–48, 52–53, 65–66; personal perspective on, 59–60; in setting direction, 50–51, 56; summary of capacities and, 56; summary of interpersonal influence capacities and, 90; ways of addressing, 60–61; in Zoffner case study, 49, 51, 59, 60–61, 65–66
Personal experience, authority through, 58–59
Personal hopes and dreams, 137–138
Personal responsibility, 162–165
Perspectives: in cross-functional, self-managed team, 112–124; in diverse organization, 106–107; in flattened organization, 105–106; integration of, by interpersonal influence leader, 79–81, 85–88, 91–92, 95–96, 98–100, 125–126; of leader as being open to question and doubt, 79–80, 86–87, 88; leader as container for, 78, 88; leader as repository for differing, 80–81, 85–86, 88, 91–92, 108; learning from, 107. See also Worldviews
Pharaohs, 57–58
Physics, 145
Picture, 25
Planning cycles, 107
Political boundaries, acknowledgment of shared work across, 130
Polysemous tools, 25
Pope, 58
Postmodern context, 109, 126–134
Power: in leadership versus management, 80; sources of, in interpersonal influence principle, 72
Principles versus definitions, 7–10. See also Knowledge principles; Leadership principles
Privileged voices, 101–102
Problem-solving versus sensemaking mind-set, 157–159
Problem statements, 157–158
Psychological development, limits of personal dominance principle and, 49, 59–60

**Q**

Quantum mechanics, 143, 145

**R**

Race, perspectives on, 146
Rationalism, age of, 58
Reality: found versus relationally constructed, 139–144; relationally constructed, 135–165. See also Relational dialogue
Reciprocity: in interpersonal influence principle, 108; in personal dominance principle, 40, 41–42, 43, 48–49, 52–53, 60–61, 65–66; in shared knowledge principles, 31–32

Relational dialogue (third leadership principle), 12, 125–165; adaptive challenge and, 26; approaches to bringing forth, 155–165; commitment and, 25–26; compared with other leadership principles, 151–154; construction of reality in, 135–139; contexts that call for, 125–134; dialogue in, as making sense of a new subject, 144–149; dialogue in, developing the capacity for, 160–162; direction setting and, 25; as the embedding principle, 12, 151–155; equal worth of differing worldviews in, 131–132, 139, 142–143; examples of contexts that call for, 127–129; examples of contexts that call for, common elements of, 129–134; leaders and leadership in, 133–134, 139–144; for leadership across worldviews, 139–165; leadership as process of shared meaning-making in, 149–151, 152–155; leadership tasks and, 25–26, 132–133, 140, 144, 149, 151–155; mutual acknowledgment of shared work in, 129–131, 132; narrative mode for, 159–160; overview of, 14–15; responsibility in, 162–165; sensemaking processes for, 156–159; summary of contexts calling for, 134; truths in-the-making of, 15, 134–151; in Zoffner case study, 167–173

Relational processes: construction of reality within, 135–165. See also Relational dialogue

Relativity, 145, 146, 147

Responsibility: accountability versus, 163–164; in relational dialogue principle, 162–165

Rost, J. C., 107

Rulers, 57–58

**S**

Second leadership principle. See Interpersonal influence

Self, relational construction of, 135–137

Self-doubt, 31–32

Self-managed teams, 96–97, 111–116; developmental tasks of, 112; leadership of, 113; leadership tasks in, 112–122; unity masking diversity in, 116–124

Senior-level management: changing work of, 105–106; sensemaking work of, 156–159

Sensemaking: cultivating processes of, 156–159; future search conference for, in Zoffner case study, 170–173; leadership as process of shared, 149–151; narrative and, 159–160; problem solving versus, 157–159

*Sensemaking in Organizations* (Weick), 108

Sensemaking meetings, 158–159

Setting direction. See Direction setting (leadership task)

Shared knowledge principles. See Knowledge principles; Leadership principles

Shared vision, 118–119

Shared work. See Work, shared

Social control, 8–9

Social influence, 67–68. See also Interpersonal influence

*Social Psychology* (Allport), 8–9

"Sociological Note on Leadership" (Gerth and Mills), 10

Solomon, 57–58

Sportsmanship, 147–148

Structural change, as limiting context for interpersonal influence principle, 102–108

Subjects, new, creating and making sense of, 144–149

Succession planning, 34

Suppliers, collaborative relationships with, 103–104

Sustainable development, 146

Symbol, 25

Systemic capacity, leadership development as, 165

Systemic view of leadership, 26–30

**T**

Taken-for-granted truths. See Truths taken-for-granted

Tarot cards, 142

Tasks, leadership. See Leadership tasks

Telecommunications company example, 127, 133, 157–158

Television sports, 147–148

Third leadership principle. See Relational dialogue

Thoughts and actions, as ways of recognizing leadership, 4–7, 27–28

Transformation, relational dialogue and, 25–26. *See also* Relational dialogue
Truman, H., 69–70
Truth: differing worldviews and, 125–165; objective and subjective, 67–68, 135–140. *See also* Worldviews
Truths in-the-making: for relational dialogue principle, 135–151; truths taken-for-granted versus, 134–135
Truths taken-for-granted, 32; of interpersonal influence principle, 14, 65–77, 97–98, 110; knowledge principles and, 12; of personal dominance principle, 13, 32–36; of relational dialogue principle, 15, 134–151; truths in-the-making versus, 134–135
Turf battles, 118

**U**

U.S. politics, 130
Unity embracing diversity, 98–100, 106–107, 108–110, 113–115; versus unity masking diversity, 116–124
Universal truths, 143
Unknown-but-shared future, 25–26. *See also* Relational dialogue

**V**

Vision, penetrating, 141

**W**

Ways of knowing, 140–141, 152
*Ways of Worldmaking* (Goodman), 125
Weick, K. E., 108, 158
Whole system, leadership development at level of, 164–165
Women, views of, 146
Women's Christian Temperance Union, 37
Work: organizing around, 104–107, 108–110; senior management, 105–106
Work, shared: leadership tasks and multiple perspectives on, 132–133, 151–155; mutual acknowledgment of, as context for relational dialogue, 129–131, 132
Worldviews, 125–165; comparing, 142–143; creating new subjects from, 144–149; differing, as contexts for

relational dialogue principle, 126–134; emergence of leaders and leadership within or across, 133–134; equal worth of differing, 131–132, 139, 142–143; interpersonal influence and, 24, 67–68, 78–84, 95, 98–100, 106–110, 125–126; leadership across, as dialogue that makes sense of a new subject, 144–149; leadership across, as requiring relational dialogue, 139–144; leadership principles' approaches to, compared, 125–126; leadership tasks across, 151–155; mutual acknowledgment of shared work across differing, 129–131, 132; personal dominance and, 37–38; relational dialogue and, 14–15, 25, 26, 125–165; space between, 140–141; unity embracing diversity of, 98–100, 106–107, 108–110; unity masking diversity of, 116–124. *See also* Perspectives

**Z**

Zoffner Piano Company (case study): adaptive challenges in, 42–44, 53–54; commitment in, under interpersonal influence principle, 86; commitment in, under personal dominance principle, 41–42, 52–53; cross-functional, self-managed team of, 96–97, 112–116, 119–122; culture clash in, 95–96; customer definition in, 169–170; digital piano issue in, 15–18, 42–44, 53–54, 73–74, 77, 94, 95, 116–117, 167–173; direction setting in, under interpersonal influence principle, 84–85; direction setting in, under personal dominance principle, 39–40, 51; Elena introduced in, 2–3; Elena's adaptive challenge task in, 44–47; Elena's succession to leadership in, 15–18, 31–32, 49, 61; Elena's transition to interpersonal influence in, 63–64, 66–67, 71, 73–77, 78–79, 82–84, 93–94; founding of, 1–2; future search retreat of, 170–173; interpersonal influence limits in, 93–97, 111–116, 119–122; interpersonal influence principle in, 63–64, 65–66, 73–77, 78–79, 82–85, 86; introduced,

1–3; leadership principles in, 29, 30; leadership task problems in, 19; Mr. Karl's leadership of, 1–3, 4, 6, 12–13, 23, 31–32, 35–36, 39–40, 41, 42, 59, 60–61, 65–66, 71; Mr. Karl's leadership tasks in, 35–36, 39–40, 41; Mr. Karl's retirement from, 15–18, 31–32, 41, 65–66; Musitron division of, 94–97, 114–116, 119–122, 167–173; personal dominance principle in, 12, 23, 30, 31–32, 35–36, 39–40, 41, 42–44, 49, 51, 53–54, 60–61, 65–66; relational dialogue principle in, 167–173

# About the Author

**Wilfred Drath** is group director of New Lenses on Leadership and a senior fellow at the Center for Creative Leadership in Greensboro, North Carolina. He has studied leaders and managers and how they develop and has participated in leadership development design over the last seventeen years. His current research and educational work focuses on the evolution of leadership in the knowledge age. He has authored or coauthored publications including *Making Common Sense: Leadership as Meaning-Making in a Community of Practice; Evolving Leaders: A Model for Promoting Leadership Development in Programs; Beyond Ambition: How Driven Managers Can Lead Better and Live Better;* and *Approaching the Future of Leadership Development*.

Before joining CCL in 1979, he worked in numerous jobs—bus driver, truck driver, kitchen manager, policeman, pipe fitter, store detective, teacher, editor, free-lance writer, photographer, and filmmaker. He was eventually granted an AB in English by the University of Georgia and then spent a couple of wonderful but non-degree-earning years in graduate school at the University of North Carolina in Chapel Hill.

He is married and has three children.

He likes golf.

# More Titles from the <u>Center</u> for Creative Leadership

## Leadership in Action
### Martin Wilcox, Editor

Keep yourself up to date on the latest leadership research and practices. *Leadership in Action* offers readers the latest findings from CCL's many ongoing research projects and expert advice on how these can best be applied in the real world. Published bimonthly, each issue delivers in-depth articles designed to help practicing leaders hone their existing skills and identify and develop new ones.

One year (six issues) individual rate: $99.00
One year (six issues) institutional rate: $124.00

---

## Maximizing the Value of 360-Degree Feedback
### *A Process for Successful Individual and Organizational Development*
### Walter Tornow, Manuel London, & CCL Associates

In this volume, CCL draws upon twenty-eight years of leading research and professional experience to deliver the most thorough, practical, and accessible guide to 360-degree feedback ever. Readers will discover precisely how they can use 360-degree feedback as a tool for achieving a variety of objectives such as communicating performance expectations, setting developmental goals, establishing a learning culture, and tracking the effects of organizational change. Detailed guidelines show how 360-degree feedback can be designed to maximize employee involvement, self-determination, and commitment. Filled with case examples and a full complement of instructive instruments.

Hardcover   320 pages   ISBN 0-7879-0958-0   Item #F093   $44.95

"*This wonderfully useful guide to leadership development will prove an invaluable resource to anyone interested in growing the talent of their organizations.*"
—Jay A. Conger, professor, USC, and author of *Learning to Lead*

### The Center for Creative Leadership
### *Handbook of Leadership Development*
**Cynthia D. McCauley, Russ S. Moxley, Ellen Van Velsor, Editors**

In one comprehensive volume, the Center for Creative Leadership distills its philosophy, findings, and methodologies into a practical resource that sets a new standard in the field. Filled with proven techniques and detailed instructions for designing and enabling the most effective leadership development programs possible—including six developed by CCL itself—this is the ultimate professional guide from the most prestigious organization in the field.

Hardcover   512 pages   ISBN 0-7879-0950-5   Item #F116   $70.00

---

"*At last, a practical, quick, direct, and easy-to-use tool that helps individuals flex their learning muscles! I'll use the Learning Tactics Inventory (LTI) in my consulting practice right away.*"
—Beverly Kaye, author, *Up Is Not the Only Way*

### Learning Tactics Inventory
### *Facilitator's Guide & Participant's Workbook*
**Maxine Dalton**

Developed by CCL, the Learning Tactics Inventory (LTI) gives you everything you need to conduct a two- to four-hour workshop that dramatically enhances participants' ability to learn. It shows each individual how he or she learns best and how each can adopt new learning strategies accordingly. The *Inventory* is used by workshop participants to profile individual learning styles. The *Participant's Workbook* is used to score and interpret results. The *Facilitator's Guide*, which includes a sample copy of the *Participant's Workbook*, details all key workshop procedures—including setup, administration, and follow-up—and comes with reproducible overhead and handout masters. You'll need one Inventory and Workbook per participant. Available at bulk discounts.

LTI Inventory   paperback   48 pages   Item #G515   $12.95
LTI Facilitator's Guide [includes sample Workbook]   paperback   48 pages
Item #G514   $24.95

# Job Challenge Profile
## *Learning from Work Experience*
### Marian N. Ruderman, Cynthia D. McCauley, Patricia J. Ohlott

Increase career satisfaction and job performance among your employees with these field-tested tools that help them seek new challenges and develop valuable new skills. The *Inventory* helps individuals profile what and how much they're learning, where their key challenges lie, and how they can maximize learning in their day-to-day experiences. The *Participant's Workbook* is used to score and interpret results. The *Facilitator's Guide*, which includes a sample copy of the *Participant's Workbook*, contains complete instructions for conducting two- to four-hour workshops. The result will be the creation of a learning work environment where challenge is welcome and job fulfillment is high.

JCP Instrument  6 pages  Item #G108  $4.95
JCP Participant's Workbook  paperback  48 pages  Item #G106  $12.95
JCP Facilitator's Guide [includes sample Workbook]  paperback
48 pages  Item #G107  $24.95

---

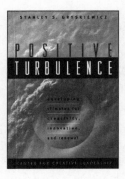

# Positive Turbulence
## *Developing Climates for Creativity, Innovation, and Renewal*
### Stanley S. Gryskiewicz

Can your company manage—even encourage—turbulence in ways that actually strengthen its competitive stance? Absolutely. In this work, top organizational psychologist Stanley Gryskiewicz argues that challenges to the status quo can be catalysts for creativity, innovation, and renewal and shows leaders how they can keep their company on the competitive edge by embracing a process he calls Positive Turbulence. Developed through the author's work with many of the world's leading companies over the course of thirty years, *Positive Turbulence* delivers proven methods for creating an organization that continuously renews itself through the committed pursuit of new ideas, products, and processes.

Hardcover  224 pages  ISBN 0-7879-1008-2  Item #E952  $32.95

# Leadership and Spirit
## *Breathing New Vitality and Energy into Individuals and Organizations*
### Russ S. Moxley

Learn how you can harness your inner spirit to help yourself and those around you approach work with a renewed sense of purpose and satisfaction. In this book, Moxley shows how spirit can spawn a more vital and vibrant kind of leadership—one that, in turn, promotes the creativity, vitality, and well-being of others. Here, Moxley examines various leadership practices: those that elevate people's spirits and those that cause the spirit to wither and wane. He offers specific suggestions on what each of us can do to reach a new level of awareness regarding leadership. And he demonstrates how a spirited leadership that values rituals, celebrations, and employee input creates a totally engaged workforce; one that brings the whole person—mental, emotional, physical, *and* spiritual—to work.

Hardcover   256 pages   ISBN 0-7879-0949-1   Item #F115-3C9   $32.95

---

# Executive Selection
## *Strategies for Success*
### Valerie I. Sessa, Jodi J. Taylor

As evinced by recent crises at Aetna, Mattel, and Citicorp, a single misstep in selecting top executives can spell trouble for the most stable of organizations. Yet the development of clear criteria for executive selection is too often pushed aside in the face of more immediate challenges. Based on Center for Creative Leadership research and the authors' extensive experience in dealing with top-level executives, this book outlines a comprehensive system for matching the right person with the right job. By answering such questions as "Who should be involved in the hiring decision?" and "How can the best candidates be identified?" this book will help ensure that your organization always enjoys quality leadership.

Hardcover   208 pages   ISBN 0-7879-5020-3   Item #G700   $34.95

# Discovering the Leader in You
## *A Guide to Realizing Your Personal Leadership Potential*

### Robert J. Lee, Sara N. King

This book is based on a simple point: leadership roles should be filled by people who deliberately decide that they want to be in them. To that end, *Discovering the Leader in You* offers a unique system of self-discovery that clearly shows how you can attain the leadership position you want. Robert J. Lee and Sara N. King, who developed this approach from their experience at the widely renowned Center for Creative Leadership, help potential leaders examine development paths in the context of who they are as individuals. They show how you can connect your inner self to the demands of leadership by using a set of questions that will help you take your career in new directions. You'll gain insight into what leadership means to you personally as you take control of your career choices and, subsequently, achieve more personal success.

Hardcover   192 pages   ISBN 0-7879-0951-3   Item #F113   $32.95